A BOOK OF BOOKS

For those who think they're "not readers" and for the parents hoping to raise little ones who are—
This is your invitation to discover the wonder that lies within the pages of a book.

First published in India by HarperCollins *Publishers* 2025
HarperCollins *Publishers* India,
Cyber City, Building 10-A, Gurugram, Haryana-122002, India
www.harpercollins.co.in

2 4 6 8 10 9 7 5 3 1

P-ISBN: 978-9369-89-729-2
E-ISBN: 978-9369-89-860-2

Cover design: Rohina Thapar
Sonali's photos by Saurabh Das, curated by 59th Parallel
Typeset in Adobe Garamond Pro 12pt

Printed and bound at
Thomson Press (India) Ltd

*

HarperCollins Publishers, Macken House, 39/40 Mayor Street Upper,
Dublin 1, D01 C9W8, Ireland

A BOOK OF BOOKS

SONALi BENDRE BEHL

DESiGNED BY ROHiNA THAPAR

HarperCollins *Publishers* India

1

TH1RTEEN R3ASONS WHY EVERYONE SHOULD READ

A reader lives a thousand lives before he dies.
The man who never reads lives only once.

- George R.R. Martin

Remember when you were a little child and a teacher read to you from a huge storybook while you and all your little friends sat on the rug, listening in rapt attention as a fantastic world came alive for you?

All of us have a similar memory from our play school or nursery or kindergarten. The world may have changed a lot since we were children, but the one thing that has not changed is our fascination with stories. Tell a story and you have the audience eating out of your hand. This is true of every audience, irrespective of age, gender or culture.

**We all love a good story.
And stories live within books.**

Our love for stories dates back a long, long time. This explains the fascination in the olden days with the wandering minstrels, the bards, the kathputliwallahs, the puppet shows, and so on. Their arrival in the village or town was an event in an age when there weren't that many avenues for entertainment. This also explains the popularity of our epics – the *Ramayana* and the *Mahabbharata*.

MANY OF US HAVE GROWN UP HEARING OUR GRANDMOTHERS AND GRANDFATHERS TELL US STORIES TO WHILE AWAY THE LONG WINTER EVENINGS.

They came down to us through the oral tradition and then through the written word and even today we love reading them as presented to us by modern-day writers. In fact, these two Indian epics, like the Greek epics Homer's *Iliad* and *Odyssey*, are like a baggy monster of a book containing various stories linked together with a central storyline.

From the day we learn the alphabet and recognize the pronunciation, the sound of each letter, we become a reader. Many of us have grown up hearing our grandmothers and grandfathers tell us stories to while away the long winter evenings. Though we didn't realize it then, all this was catering to a basic human need, the need to listen raptly to a good story.

SO, WHY SHOULD WE READ?

TH1RTEEN REASONS WHY

1 To be entertained

Stories provide entertainment first and foremost. Books are exciting because of the wide variety of stories they offer that take you to wonderful worlds and imaginative settings that vary from story to story and book to book.

2 To be transported to new worlds

When you open the pages of a book, you feel a sense of anticipation that almost brings on the goosebumps. You know that you are going to enter a world that will envelop you and hold you within its grasp for the next few hours or days or even weeks, depending on the length of the book. Ask any child or even adult who is a fan of *Harry Potter*, what fascinates them and the most common answer you get is:
"I love living in that world."

BOOKS EXPOSE READERS TO VARIOUS IDEAS, SETTINGS AND CONCEPTS THAT CAN INFLUENCE THEIR OWN CREATIVE ENDEAVOURS.

3 To understand people and the world

Books contain ideas, thoughts, facts. Stories are a wonderful way to gain an insight into society, its people and the different cultures across the world. Books are written by people, and as such, offer a diversity of perspectives and worldviews, which reflect the culture and heritage of the writer. Being exposed to these varied ways of seeing the world helps us understand it better.

4 To broaden one's horizons

Books are a rich source of information and knowledge on various subjects, including history, science, philosophy, self-help and much more. Reading books helps individuals broaden their horizons and stay informed about the world.

5 To inspire creativity

Books expose readers to various ideas, settings, and concepts that can influence their own creative endeavours. And the more books we read, the more creative we become, not only with our words, but also with the things we can imagine.

6 To improve communication and analytical skills

Reading books exposes you to words, sentences and the creative use of language such as idioms, metaphors, similes and more that will help improve your spoken language. It also enhances your analytical and problem-solving skills.

READING BOOKS HELPS INDIVIDUALS BROADEN THEIR HORIZONS AND STAY INFORMED ABOUT THE WORLD.

7 To build vocabulary and language comprehension

Reading enhances vocabulary and language comprehension, which makes writing easier. Exposure to diverse writing styles and word usage expands the possibilities that language offers us, giving us different ways of expressing our thoughts.

8 To experience personal growth

Every time we read a book, we experience personal growth, expand our knowledge, and see cognitive development. When it comes to self-help and personal development, books can provide valuable insights and offer practical advice on how to overcome challenges, set goals and lead fulfilling and rich lives.

9 To build imagination

Reading also helps stimulate the brain. It is a kind of yoga for the brain cells. It challenges the mind, improves concentration, and helps prevent cognitive decline, especially as people grow older.

EVERY TIME
WE READ A BOOK,
WE EXPERIENCE
PERSONAL GROWTH,
EXPAND OUR
KNOWLEDGE,
AND SEE COGNITIVE
DEVELOPMENT.

10 To concentrate and focus better

Reading requires concentration and focus, which can transfer to other areas of life and improve productivity. So not only does reading sharpen one's brain and focus, but you will also find that you work much better after taking a reading break. It is akin to F1 cars making a pit stop.

11 To become empathetic

Stories allow readers to immerse themselves in the perspectives and experiences of different characters, promoting understanding of others. They allow you to put yourself in the shoes of others and grow your capacity for empathy.

12 To relax and reduce stress

Engaging with a good book can be a great way to relax and reduce stress. Reading offers an escape from everyday worries and allows the mind to unwind.

13 To sleep better

Reading before bedtime can improve sleep quality by reducing stress and providing a calming pre-sleep routine. This is why parents read to children before bedtime. This is true for adults too. Picking up a book before going to sleep will help you wind down, offering you the opportunity for a good night's rest.

While reading books offers numerous benefits, it's essential to remember that everyone has different preferences. Some may prefer audiobooks, while others enjoy e-books or physical copies. The key is to find what works best for you and make reading a regular part of your life to reap the many rewards it offers.

An inscription over the earliest authenticated library belonging to Pharaoh Ramses II, stated that it was a house of healing for the soul. It inspired people so much that in 1760 when the beautiful baroque library at the Abbey of St. Gall in St. Gallen, Switzerland, was renovated, the inscription in Greek was placed over the entrance to the main hall – "Healing place for the soul".

AND MORE!

What is an epic?

An epic is a long narrative poem that recounts the heroic deeds and adventures of a legendary or mythological figure. Epics often serve as a means of preserving and conveying cultural, moral, and historical values. These poems are characterized by their grand scale, elevated language, and the incorporation of supernatural elements, gods, and heroic feats.

One of the most well-known examples of an epic is Homer's *Iliad* and *Odyssey*, which are ancient Greek poems celebrating the heroes and events surrounding the Trojan War. Other examples include the *Epic of Gilgamesh* from Mesopotamian literature, Dante's *Divine Comedy* and, of course, the Indian epic poems *Mahabharata* and *Ramayana*.

READiNG LOG

Books I've read recently

Title ....

Author ....

Rating for the book ♡♡♡♡♡

Summary ....

....

....

Title ....

Author ....

Rating for the book ♡♡♡♡♡

Summary ....

....

....

Title ....

Author ....

Rating for the book ♡♡♡♡♡

Summary ....

....

....

Title ....

Author ....

Rating for the book ♡♡♡♡♡

Summary ....

....

....

Title ....

Author ....

Rating for the book ♡♡♡♡♡

Summary ....

....

....

2

FORTY RULES OF LOVING READING

How To Become A Book Lover

Becoming a book lover is a personal process of evolution. The key is to find what works best for you and make reading an integral part of your life. Reading can be a lifelong, fulfilling hobby that opens up new worlds, stimulates your imagination and broadens your perspective.

In today's world of screens where we go to a phone or a tablet or a laptop or the television screen for everything from studying to playing to entertainment, a book offers your tired eyes some rest. You can actually feel your eyes relaxing when you pick up a book.

1 Be open to new experiences

A lively curiosity is the first trait of a book lover. That insatiable thirst for knowledge, the desire to know what happens next will make you want to keep reading. If you are new to the world of books, choose a genre that you like; not because your friend likes it. Your guide can be the kind of movies or television shows that you like to watch. If you prefer to watch comedies, there is no point in picking up a crime thriller.

IF YOU ARE NEW TO THE WORLD OF BOOKS, CHOOSE A GENRE THAT YOU LIKE.

2 Allocate a budget for books

If you are not born into a family of booklovers and readers, it is difficult to cultivate a love for books. One way is to decide that once a month you will buy a book. Spend time choosing that book. Keep a budget that you will use only to buy a book. And if you've spent time and money on buying a book, it is likely you will be inclined to read it.

3 Focus on your interests

Begin by selecting books that align with your interests. Whether you're into fiction, non-fiction, science fiction, romance, or history, choosing books that genuinely interest you will make reading more enjoyable.

4 Go for a book series

Choose a genre you like and pick up a book that is part of a series. That way if you like this first book, you will pick up the next volume to know what happens next. This is one of the reasons publishers publish book series and space them out for regular publication.

5 Opt for lighter tomes

If you are new to the world of reading, take baby steps. Do not pick up a book by Tolstoy or Dickens. Start small with romances or mysteries, for instance. Romance is among the largest-selling genres as are cozy mysteries, such as those written by Agatha Christie (Hercule Poirot or Miss Marple mysteries) or Charlaine Harris (Aurora Teagarden mysteries).

6 Be patient and keep going

If the first book does not stimulate your reading hormones, just continue. It is more than likely that after two or three books, you will find your interest growing.

START SMALL WiTH ROMANCES OR MYSTERiES.

7 Find the movie

Sometimes watching the movie helps. The world is divided into two camps – those who feel that the movie can never do justice to the book, and those who swear that movies enhance the satisfaction of reading the book. But when you have watched and loved Colin Firth as Darcy in *Pride and Prejudice* or Johnny Flynn as Knightley in *Emma*, you will find yourself drawn to the books irresistibly.

8 Create a reading space

Find a cozy and comfortable reading nook in your home where you can escape with a good book without distractions. Make this your happy place, where you go for rest, relaxation and succour.

9 Set realistic reading goals

Set achievable reading goals, whether it's a certain number of pages per day or a specific number of books per month. This can help you stay committed and track your progress.

10 Join a Book Club

Joining a book club or reading group can introduce you to new books and provide a platform for discussions, fostering a sense of community around reading. Also, you will find other readers which becomes a huge motivating factor.

11 Visit libraries and bookstores

Make a bookshop your go-to space. And make a library card. Spend time browsing in libraries and bookstores. The physical presence of books and the opportunity to discover new titles can be quite inspiring.

12 Stretch yourself and read widely

Once you have taken the first step and started reading, stretch your wings. Don't limit yourself to one genre or type of book. Read a diverse range of materials to broaden your horizon and explore different writing styles.

13 Allocate a time for reading

Allocate a specific time each day for reading. It could be in the morning, before bed, or during your daily commute. In the beginning this is a good way to create a habit. Soon you will find yourself picking up a book almost in a Pavlovian effect.

RECORD YOUR THOUGHTS AND FEELINGS ABOUT THE BOOKS YOU READ IN A JOURNAL.

14 Keep a reading journal

Journalling about what you read will help you reflect on your reading journey and make it a more personal experience. And it becomes a great resource for your next book club meeting.

15 Share your love for books

Discuss books with friends and family. Recommend your favourite books and listen to their recommendations as well. Sharing your passion for books can be contagious. And you will find a feeling of camaraderie developing among book lovers within your family and friends' circle.

16 Love your own voice

Try reading aloud, especially if you are a new reader. It can enhance your connection with the material and make the experience more enjoyable. And it will bring the book alive for you.

17 Have storytelling sessions

Host a reading evening with family or friends where each person reads aloud a section from the same book. This is a great way to grow to love books, especially when you are new to reading. It will also help speed your way through a book, especially a longer one.

18

Reading to children

As you discover the joy of books and the pleasure of reading, why not pass it on to the next generation? Read aloud to children and get more readers to follow in your footsteps. If you are a new adult reader, you might not have read many children's books and often they can be fun to discover even as grownups. Even today many adults love reading Enid Blyton's books, Louisa May Alcott's *Little Women*, Laura Ingalls Wilder's *Little House on the Prairie*, Elinor M. Brent-Dyer's *Chalet School* books and several other bestselling and well-known children's books.

19 Find a reading buddy

Just as when you join a new activity, such as the gym or other similar activities, you find it more enjoyable when you do it with a buddy. Do the same thing with books. Make a close friend a reading buddy. Sit silently and read a book side by side. That way you will have a person to discuss your reading with even if your family is far away or has no interest in reading.

20 Patronize book cafes

Grab your next coffee at a book café so that you have the option to read instead of enjoying a gossip session with a friend. The best thing about becoming a reader and a lover of books is that you will never again be bored by yourself. Your best friend is always with you, in your bag, on your iPad or your Kindle.

21 Explore different formats

Once you have been swept up by the joy of reading, explore different formats. If your preferred choice was an eBook, then opt for the physical copy and pick up a paperback from the bookstore.

THE BEST THING ABOUT BECOMING A READER IS THAT YOU WILL NEVER AGAIN BE BORED BY YOURSELF.

22 Read in a foreign language

If you speak more than one language, pick up books in the one that you don't usually read in. For example, if you love the Harry Potter series of books in English, pick up the German translation. It will increase your proficiency in German and make your reading journey more interesting.

23 Create a bucket list

Once you start reading and get an idea of what kind of books you like to read, create a bucket list of the books you want to get to. Don't make it too long or it could be demotivating. Start with five to ten books.

24 Theme challenge

Set a challenge for yourself such as reading books by a particular author or era or genre. For instance, to read three regency romances this month. Or five mysteries. Or two thrillers. Meeting a goal is always satisfying.

25 Take part in read-a-thons

Just as a buddy is great to read books with and discuss them, any community, online or face-to-face, can be motivational. One activity that is particularly fun and motivating is a read-a-thon. Even reading clubs can do this. Everyone reads a particular chapter or chapters or book in a specified time period.

26 Join online reading communities

This is another avatar of book clubs, where people can be across borders, across continents, and across ages. It makes for a more eclectic mix of people. You can join such groups on Goodreads or Reddit or Quora. Or even create one of your own.

27 Track your reading

Just as dietitians tell you to track what you eat, tracking what you read is a great way to boost your ego. You can use apps such as Goodreads, Bookly, Bookshout, LibraryThing and BookBuddy to help you track your reading, manage your books, build a lasting habit of reading and remember what you read.

28 Read books about books

Once you have developed a backlist of books you have read, it becomes interesting to read other people's views about what you have read. However, even when you are a beginning reader, reading about the genesis of nursery rhymes or Mother Goose or Grimms' Fairy Tales can be very interesting.

29 Visit literary landmarks

Just sitting with a book can be a tall ask, especially for someone who has only just started reading. But visiting a place associated with the book or the author can be an activity that will make the reading even more interesting. For instance, if you are reading Jane Austen, visiting Chawton or Bath where places associated with her books are now museums can be good fun. And if you are reading Jane Austen's *Persuasion*, a visit to the seaside resort of Lyme Regis is certainly interesting. Similarly, if you are reading Dan Brown's *Da Vinci Code*, and you happen to visit Rome or Paris, do take the Dan Brown Tour.

30 Learn the backstory

Knowing what led the author to write that particular book can enhance your enjoyment of the tale. *Murder on the Orient Express* by Agatha Christie is a book that is wonderful to read. The fascination is proved by how many great producers and directors have their own version of the book including the latest by Kenneth Branagh in 2017. But the original book was inspired by the kidnapping of distinguished aviator Charles Lindbergh's baby son. Reading about the kidnapping can lead you to other books such as James Patterson's *Along Came A Spider*, Melanie Benjamin's *The Aviator's Wife*, Maurice Sendak's *Outside Over There*, and Max Allan Collins' *Stolen Away*.

DO YOU KNOW WHO WAS RESPONSIBLE FOR LONDON BRIDGE FALLING DOWN? OR WHAT WAS THE BLACK SHEEP BAAING ABOUT?

31 Attend author events

Listening to an author speak about his or her work can give you an insight into the book. It will add another dimension to your reading and make the exercise more interesting.

32 Swap your books

Every book you read does not have to be one that you own. Exchange the books you have read with friends and others. This can be done among members of the book club, for instance. Sometimes there are places where you can 'Take a book, leave a book'. In a small village in Dorset in the United Kingdom, an old public telephone box has become a site for this. Villagers leave books they don't want any more for others to take for free. This means that the iconic red telephone booths have found a fresh lease of life as makeshift libraries.

33 Link your hobby with books

You might be new to reading but you might have other hobbies such as knitting or sewing or painting or craft or cooking. Linking this to your new hobby of reading can be a creative way to pique your interest in books. You could also get more people this way to become readers. For instance, hold a workshop where you make bookmarks and coasters based on a particular book or author. Or have a bookshelf-making competition. Or a cookery evening where you make dishes mentioned in a particular book. Or even dishes from a particular era.

34 Blogs and Vlogs

Success is meant to be shared. And reading a book or completing a series is a matter of pride, especially for new readers. Why not share it with others? Shout it out from the mountain tops! Create a blog and share your reading journey with others. You might become a role model. If you like making videos or reels, create a vlog of your love affair with books.

WHEN YOU LIKE A BOOK, YOU WANT TO KNOW MORE. YOU WANT TO KNOW WHAT MADE THE AUTHOR WRITE THE BOOK. WHAT WAS THE INSPIRATION?

35 Create fan fiction

This is a great way to remain invested in a book and to get started on your writing journey too. Take characters from a book you have read and liked, and put them in new situations, or put yourself in the world of the book. How cool would it be to exist next to your favourite characters?!

36 Interactive novels

For those who have never picked up a book, it can be quite intimidating to start reading. One way is to try out interactive novels. Or books that incorporate multimedia elements, such as hyperlinks, music, and video, to create a more immersive experience.

37 Create a playlist

Make a playlist based on your book, either on the basis of artists who belong to its setting, or the mood that the book evoked. Whenever you listen to the playlist, you will feel transported to your book and will be itching to read again. Sharing it with others will also help them get interested in the book you like so much.

38 Choose books with visuals

This is a good idea for new readers. The visuals break up the greyness of the text and introduce an element of fun as well. The comic book and graphic novel formats are especially useful for hesitant readers or readers who would rather read small bits of text that is accompanied by visuals and illustrations.

39 Book-themed parties

Instead of just hosting a dinner, base the next get-together on a book. Decorate the room according to the theme of the book and have a treasure hunt with clues based on the book. Not only will you read the book, but your guests will do so too! You would, perhaps, have turned another ten people into readers!

40 Sleep with a book

Make bedtime reading a habit. This will turn your book into almost a security blanket, offering you a feeling of safety and comfort through reading.

And finally, some people are born book lovers, some have a love for books thrust upon them. The beauty is that in either case, the person stands to gain.

AND MORE!

The development of bookshops is closely tied to the history of printing and the availability of books for purchase.

One of the earliest and most famous bookshops with historical significance is the Officina Plantiniana in Antwerp, Belgium. The Officina Plantiniana, established by Christophe Plantin in the mid-16th century, was not only a printing press but also a bookshop. It played a crucial role in the dissemination of books during the Renaissance. Another notable early bookshop is the Giunti Bookstore in Venice, Italy, founded by the Giunti family in the 16th century. The Giunti Bookstore was known for its extensive collection of books and played a major role in the publishing industry.

These early establishments, along with others, contributed to the evolution of bookshops. Over time, bookshops became integral parts of communities, promoting literacy and serving as cultural hubs.

Portuguese bookseller Livraria Bertrand's Lisbon store in Chiado was acknowledged by the Guinness Book of Records in 2011 as the oldest operating bookstore. Livraria Bertrand, which has 59 branches across the world, opened this store in 1732.

FAVOURiTES!

The books I've read

My favourite authors

My favourite series

3

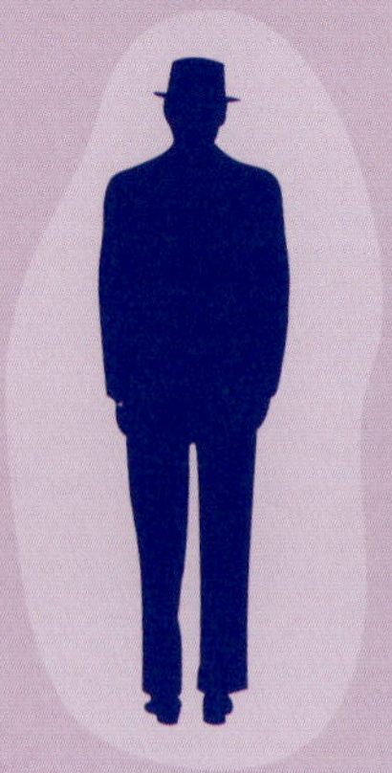

WALKiNG THROUGH READiNG WALLS

Books really do have that quality, the ability to transport you to worlds only imagined, the world of magic, the world of pixies and fairies, the world of the Faraway Tree, of adventure and thrills – a world far removed from reality.

You actually enter a world where, like Samuel Taylor Coleridge said in his *Biographia Literaria*, there is a willing suspension of disbelief, and you enjoy it more for it. In fact, the harsher the reality, the more readers want to escape into these magical worlds. This perhaps explains why the genre of romances, of 'chick lit' as they are called, flourishes during an economic slowdown or financial crisis. **Then the question is, why don't people read? What stops them?**

A major reason is that they just don't know what books can offer them. They might have non-reader parents and so were not exposed to books when they were young. Often, they would be introduced to books at school. But if they are not, they end up deprived of the promise that a book can offer. Sometimes people who come from economically challenged sections of society may simply lack access to books. They might not be able to go to libraries or other places that boast book resources.

READiNG CAN BE A MAGiC WAY TO COPE WiTH ANYTHiNG THAT LiFE THROWS AT YOU.

Happiness and sorrow, grief and joy, ecstasy and depression – books can help you get through them all. There is a book for every occasion. However, to get through the walls – virtual or real – that prevent you from reaching that goal of becoming a reader, you need some help, some friends, some buddies. Like the dwarves for Snow White in the Disney version, for example. In fact, the dwarves are representative of various situations you might go through in life or even in a day and each of them – Doc, Dopey, Sneezy, Bashful, Grumpy, Sleepy and Happy – can be the one to hold your hand to get through it – as though each came with his own brand of books. Let's list how each dwarf can help you find the right books in each situation.

1 Doc

As the leader of the group, Doc might recommend a diverse range of genres based on the individual's interests and needs. He would likely take a thoughtful approach, considering the reader's preferences and offering tailored recommendations. Non-fiction books on various topics such as history, science or philosophy could expand the reader's horizons, while self-help books on personal development or leadership might inspire growth and introspection. He also tends to mix up things when excited, so books on puzzles or crosswords would fall under his purview. He is very kind and nurturing too so he might recommend books on self-care, baby development and parenting.

2 Dopey

While Dopey is a dwarf that never speaks, he doesn't let that get in the way of his ability to communicate. He is also the one who first accepts Snow White completely and unconditionally as seen from the way he runs back inside to get an extra kiss from her before going off to work. Dopey's playful and whimsical nature suggests that he would enjoy genres that spark his imagination and sense of wonder. Children's literature with colorful illustrations and magical stories such as the *Winnie the Pooh* series and the Dr Seuss books could captivate his attention. Additionally, fantasy tales filled with mythical creatures and enchanting worlds might transport him to realms of fantasy and adventure. Authors like J.K. Rowling, Roald Dahl, or C.S. Lewis could offer delightful reads for someone like Dopey.

3 Sneezy

Apart from his gigantic sneezes, Sneezy is a dwarf who is quick to jump to conclusions. This is seen when he believed that someone had stolen their dishes when he saw the empty sink. Sneezy's tendency to sneeze frequently might indicate a need for excitement and stimulation. He might enjoy genres that are fast-paced and adrenaline-fuelled. If you're like Sneezy, you probably enjoy adventurous or action-packed genres that keep you on the edge of your seat. Fantasy novels with epic adventures, thrillers with gripping suspense, or adventure stories could cater to your desire for excitement. Authors like Lee Child or Dan Brown might provide you with the thrill you seek in a good book like Sneezy.

4 Bashful

Bashful is a dwarf who is so shy he can barely look Snow White in the eye. His quiet but sweet nature is what makes him so endearing. He is also introspective which suggests that he might enjoy genres that delve into the complexities of human emotions and relationships. Literary fiction with rich character development and deep explorations of the human condition could resonate with him. Coming-of-age stories or emotional dramas that tackle themes of identity, love, and personal growth would capture his interest. Lucy Montgomery's *Anne of Green Gables*, Louisa May Alcott's *Little Women*, *Good Wives*, *Little Men* and *Jo's Boys*, Charles Dickens' *David Copperfield, Great Expectations* etc., could be compelling reads for someone like Bashful.

5 Grumpy

Grumpy is characterized by his skepticism and no-nonsense attitude. He values practicality and tends to be a bit cynical. He is a character that so many of us can relate to. If we look around us, we all know or knew someone similar to Grumpy. He is unwilling to accept Snow White at first, but once he does, he is her staunchest ally. For someone like Grumpy, who might be initially resistant to the idea of reading for leisure, recommending genres that align with his practicality could be beneficial. Crime novels or detective stories with complex plots and realistic characters might appeal to his sense of logic and intrigue. He might enjoy authors like Agatha Christie, whose work is known for its clever twists.

6 Sleepy

Sleepy's tendency to doze off easily is a skill that so many might be jealous of. The ability to sleep anytime and anywhere is so valuable to those of us that get caught up in the hustle and bustle of our day-to-day lives and forget how important it is to rest. Sleepy might prefer genres that are easy to digest and don't require too much mental effort. Light-hearted comedies or cozy mysteries with simple, straightforward plots could keep him engaged without overwhelming him. Additionally, non-fiction books on topics like mindfulness, relaxation techniques, or even sleep science could provide him with valuable knowledge while catering to his need for relaxation.

7 Happy

Happy is the dwarf that is easiest to relate to. His sunny nature indicates he's sociable and easygoing, the kind of person that people are happy to be around. Happy's cheerful disposition suggests that he would gravitate towards genres that are light reads and leave readers feeling uplifted. Romance novels with heartwarming love stories, feel-good comedies that make readers laugh or inspirational fiction that explores themes of hope and resilience could make for excellent recommendations by him. Authors like Nicholas Sparks, Sophie Kinsella or Fredrik Backman might work for those who are trying to be more like Happy.

What the seven dwarves represent, encompasses almost all experiences that we go through in life and these recommendations provide a deeper insight into each personality type and the genres that might resonate with them.

THESE BOOKS CAN SERVE AS OUR WALKING STICK, GUIDING US TOWARDS OUR GOAL OF LEADING A HAPPIER AND MORE FULFILLED LIFE THROUGH READING.

Like the varied personalities of the seven dwarves, one of the great things about reading and books is that they are accessible to everyone. Whether it is different moods, attention spans, or even tiny preferences like how one likes holding a tome and turning a page, there's a book for all of this and more.

As literature seeks to unite people through exposing them to different perspectives and experiences, it becomes all the more important for it to be able to do so for everyone irrespective of their abilities.

Today, both authors and publishers are trying to be inclusive and creating books that can be accessible to everyone. In the last century, the maximum that was being done in terms of making books accessible was publishing volumes with a larger script and Braille editions. Now, however, there are audio books that can help the visually impaired, eBooks, tactile books, and those that are designed keeping autistic sensitivity to light and colour in mind. This is a great advance in the field of literature and something that is getting even better day by day.

The differently-abled face various challenges in reading books. These challenges can be influenced by the type and severity of the disability. Here are some common challenges and potential solutions:

1 Visual Impairment

Challenge: People with visual impairment may struggle with traditional printed materials.

Solution: Accessible formats such as audiobooks, Braille books, large-print books, and electronic texts with screen readers can enhance the reading experience.

2 Dyslexia

Challenge: Dyslexia can affect reading fluency, comprehension and spelling.

Solution: Specialized reading programmes, audiobooks and using fonts and backgrounds that are dyslexia-friendly can aid individuals with dyslexia.

3 Attention Deficit Hyperactivity Disorder (ADHD)

Challenge: Difficulty in paying sustained attention and focusing on reading tasks.

Solution: Breaking down reading into smaller segments, using tools like text-to-speech software and incorporating multi-sensory learning approaches can be helpful.

4 Physical Disabilities

Challenge: Difficulty holding books or turning pages due to physical limitations.

Solution: eBooks, audiobooks and adaptive devices like page turners or voice-controlled devices can facilitate reading for individuals with physical disabilities.

5 Cognitive Disabilities

Challenge: Difficulty processing and understanding information.

Solution: Simplifying language, providing visual aids and incorporating interactive and engaging learning materials can support individuals with cognitive disabilities.

6 Learning Disabilities

Challenge: Challenges in acquiring and processing written language.

Solution: Personalized learning plans, assistive technologies and individualized support can address the specific needs of individuals with learning disabilities.

7 Limited Literacy Skills

Challenge: Some differently-abled individuals may have limited literacy skills.

Solution: Literacy programmes with tailored instructional materials and one-on-one support can help build and improve their skills.

8 Social Stigma

Challenge: Social attitudes and stigma can impact differently-abled individuals' confidence and willingness to engage with reading.

Solution: Promoting inclusivity, awareness campaigns and creating supportive environments can help combat social stigma.

Even if all the challenges are overcome and the person has become a reader, he or she can go through a reading slump for some reason or the other. How do you come out of that? Many of the solutions are akin to those offered to help start reading. However, a failsafe solution is to go back to books that you read when you were a child, when you were happy, when you were looking forward to life and the future. **So, pick up that Enid Blyton or Harry Potter or Ruskin Bond book and you will be out of your reading slump within a short while.**

...GO BACK TO BOOKS THAT YOU READ WHEN YOU WERE A CHILD, WHEN YOU WERE HAPPY, WHEN YOU WERE LOOKING FORWARD TO LIFE AND THE FUTURE.

MEMORIES OF READING AND BOOKS

Why I read

My earliest memories of reading

Books that were read to me as a child

A book that I would read again

Books that are on my TBR list

4

FiFTY SHADES OF BOOKS

Books Over Time

It is difficult to visualize a world where there are no books. As stated earlier, human beings love a good story. And in today's world, stories reside predominantly within books. From the oral tradition it was a natural progression to books once writing was invented.

Even the pictorial script from ancient Egypt or Mesopotamia or China, which has the oldest history of writing, tells stories. From bones to stone to metal and papyrus, the materials used to write on kept developing but the book as we know it today came into its own when sheets or pages were compiled into a bundle in a codex format. These started playing a major role in the development of human civilization after the invention of the printing press by Johannes Gutenberg in the 15th century. The German inventor and craftsman created the movable type printing press. However, unknown to him, movable type printing was already extant in East Asia, developed after the invention of paper in the 1st century CE. The first movable type printing was seen in China around 1041-1048 CE.

Historians more or less agree on the first books being the papyrus scrolls created by ancient Egyptians. Papyrus was an ideal material for the Egyptians as it was made using the tall reeds that flourished in the Nile Valley. Individual sheets of papyrus were glued or sewn together to make scrolls. A standard scroll was around 30 feet long and 7 to 10 inches wide, while the longest Egyptian scroll ever found stretched to more than 133 feet.

By the 6th century BC, papyrus was popular throughout the Mediterranean and was used by the Greeks and Romans. Many ancient civilizations housed their scrolls in large libraries. The Royal Library of Alexandria boasted around half a million scrolls in its collection, accounting for 30-70 per cent of all books existing at the time, according to some scholars.

As papyrus grew in Egypt's Nile Valley, the Egyptians had a virtual monopoly over the papyrus trade. The rest of the world was growing tired of this and began looking for other materials. And thus, came parchment into our lives. Parchment was made from treated animal skins that were scraped thin to create a flexible and even surface. Parchment was more durable than papyrus, and it was possible to write on both sides. Also, its trade was more egalitarian. Its spread coincided with another crucial development in the history of the book. Between the 2nd and 4th centuries, the Romans began sewing folded sheets of papyrus or parchment together and binding them between wooden covers. This codex format has essentially the same structure as today's books.

The codex was much more user-friendly than the papyrus scrolls, and it was easier to carry around, easier to store and handle and easier and cheaper to produce. It also allowed readers to quickly flip between sections. The scroll remained the dominant form, however, for secular works for several centuries. The codex was the preferred form for early Christian texts, and the spread of Christianity eventually brought it into dominance.

BY THE 6TH CENTURY CE, CODEX HAD ALMOST ENTIRELY REPLACED THE SCROLL.

Block printing on paper began in China around 700 CE, though it wouldn't arrive in Europe for nearly 800 years. The first known examples of text printed on paper are tiny, 2.5-inch-wide scrolls of Buddhist prayers commissioned by Japan's Empress Shōtoku in 764 CE. The earliest example of a dated, printed book is a Buddhist text called the Diamond Sutra (868 CE).

Woodblock printing was a meticulous process that involved carving an entire page of text onto a wooden block, then inking and pressing the block to print a page.

In medieval Europe, book culture was dominated by monasteries, where monks laboriously copied and decorated texts by hand. Many of the classical texts that have survived today owe their preservation to the monks, who thought of scholarship, even the study of secular and pre-Christian writers, as a way to get closer to God. The hand-copied books were much more ornate than the mass-produced specimens of today. The degree of embellishment depended on the book's intended use and the wealth of its owner. Medieval manuscripts were so highly valued that some scribes placed threats at the beginning of the books, warning that anyone who stole or defaced the copy would be cursed.

Written in a copy of the Vulgate Bible, for example, is this warning:

> **"Whoever steals this book let him die the death; let be him be frizzled in a pan; may the falling sickness rage within him; may he be broken on the wheel and be hanged."**

The Arnstein Bible at the British Library, written in Germany around 1172, has a similar torture for the book thief: "If anyone steals it: may he die, may he be roasted in a frying pan, may the falling sickness [i.e. epilepsy] and fever attack him, and may he be rotated [on the breaking wheel] and hanged. Amen." A 15th century French curse warns:

"WHOEVER STEALS THIS BOOK WILL HANG ON A GALLOWS IN PARIS, AND, IF HE ISN'T HUNG, HE'LL DROWN, AND, IF HE DOESN'T DROWN, HE'LL ROAST, AND, IF HE DOESN'T ROAST, A WORSE END WILL BEFALL HIM."

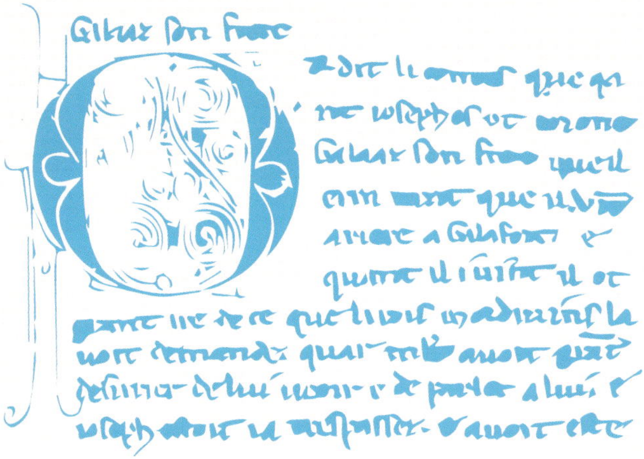

Though illuminated books were highly prized, they were also expensive and labour-intensive. By the end of the Middle Ages, the papal library in Avignon, France, held only a few thousand manuscripts compared to the nearly half-million texts found at the Library of Alexandria in ancient times. Bookmaking in the Western world became somewhat less expensive when paper emerged as the primary writing surface. Making paper from rags and other fibres, a technique that originated in 2nd century China, reached the Islamic world in the 8th century and led to the flourishing of the book culture. By the 12th century, Marrakesh in Morocco was said to have had a street lined with a hundred booksellers. But it wasn't until the 14th century that paper manufacturing began in earnest in Europe.

The Gutenberg Bible was the first book to be printed by the German inventor on his movable type press. He printed 135 copies on paper and 83 copies on vellum. This paved the way for the mass production of books. By the end of the 15th century, about 50 years after Gutenberg's invention of movable type, printing shops had sprung up throughout Europe, with an estimated 300 in Germany alone. Gutenberg's invention was a resounding success, and the printing and selling of books boomed.

Now more books were available at a lower cost, and the growth of international trade allowed them to have a wider reach. The desire for knowledge among the growing middle class and the new availability of classical texts from ancient Greece and Rome helped fuel the Renaissance, a period of celebration of the individual and the rise of humanism. For the first time, texts could be widely dispersed, allowing political, intellectual, religious and cultural ideas to spread.

Also, for the first time, many could read the same books and be exposed to the same ideas at the same time. This was the rise of mass media and mass culture that improved communication and technological and intellectual ideas spread more quickly, enabling scientists from disparate areas to build on the breakthroughs and successes of others. As the Renaissance progressed, the size of the middle class grew, as did literacy rates. Books were available to people outside monasteries or university settings, which meant increased access to books for women. In effect, the mass production of books made knowledge more democratic. This also led to resistance especially by the Roman Catholic Church which felt its control was slipping. In 1487, only a few decades after Gutenberg first printed his Bible, Pope Innocent VIII insisted that all books be pre-screened by church authorities before being printed. One book the church banned was the Bible printed in any language other than Latin – a language that was restricted to clerical or scholarly circles.

In 1517, Martin Luther instigated the Protestant Reformation. He challenged the church's authority by insisting that people had the right to read the Bible in their own language. The church rightly feared the spread of vernacular Bibles; the more people had access to the text, the less control the church was able to exert over how it was interpreted. Since the church's interpretation of the Bible dictated how people lived their lives, the church's sway over the hearts and minds of the faithful was severely undermined by accessible printed Bibles and the wave of Protestantism they encouraged. The Catholic Church's attempt to control the printing industry proved impossible to maintain, and over the next few centuries, the church would see its power decline significantly, as it was no longer the sole keeper of religious knowledge as it had been throughout the Middle Ages.

THE HIGH VALUE PLACED ON HUMAN KNOWLEDGE DURING THE RENAISSANCE LED LIBRARIES TO FLOURISH.

The Bible wasn't the only text that was beginning to be published in languages other than Latin. The Renaissance saw a growing interest in texts published in the language of the common people. The high value placed on human knowledge during the Renaissance led libraries to flourish. Libraries were a way of displaying national power and wealth. The German State Library in Berlin was founded in 1661, the National Library of Spain in Madrid in 1711, and the British Library in London in 1759. The United Kingdom's Public Libraries Act of 1850 fostered the development of free, public lending libraries. After the American Civil War, public libraries flourished in the newly reunified United States. Philanthropist Andrew Carnegie helped found more than 1,700 public libraries between 1881 and 1919.

As books became more easily available, people wanted to read books written in their native tongue. Genres with popular appeal, such as plays and poetry, became increasingly widespread. In the 16th and 17th centuries, inexpensive chapbooks became popular. Chapbooks, which derives its name from cheap books, included popular ballads, humorous stories or religious tracts. The proliferation of chapbooks showed how the Gutenberg Revolution had transformed the written word. Books were no longer considered sacred objects.

MOVE TO THE 21ST CENTURY AND BOOKS HAVE CHANGED EVEN FURTHER TO ADAPT TO THE DIGITAL AGE BRINGING EBOOKS AND AUDIOBOOKS INTO OUR LIVES.

Though the concept of an eBook was developed in the 1930s, it really came into the public arena in 1998 when eBook readers were launched and the US Congress began offering free eBooks to the public. The real gamechanger was the release of Kindle by Amazon. This was followed by the Nook by Barnes and Noble and the iPad by Apple. Today the eBook market is worth more than $10 billion.

When Thomas Edison invented the phonograph in 1877, phonographic books was something that he envisioned – books that "would speak to blind people without effort on their part". However, it would take a couple of centuries before the audiobook would become popular among the masses. With the spread of the Internet to consumers in the 1990s, faster download speeds, new compressed audio formats and portable media players, the popularity of audiobooks increased significantly during the late 1990s and 2000s. Today the global audiobook market is estimated at $5,095 million (in 2022) and expected to reach $42,268 million by 2031.

THE HISTORY OF BOOKS AND PUBLISHING IN INDIA IS DEEPLY ROOTED IN THE COUNTRY'S ANCIENT CULTURE AND TRADITIONS.

In India, books and publishing are relatively recent because of the rich oral tradition that the subcontinent has and which is strong and well-developed enough to become a civilizational link that survives to this day. Also, the pluralism as far as scripts and languages are concerned made it a challenging scene for the development of printed books.

The history of books in India is deeply rooted in the country's ancient culture and traditions. The earliest form of written communication in India can be traced back to the Vedic period (1500–500 BCE), with the oral transmission of texts like the Vedas.

These texts were later written down on palm leaves and birch bark using ancient scripts like Brahmi and Kharosthi.

During the Gupta Empire (320–550 CE), classical Sanskrit literature flourished, and important works like the *Mahabharata*, the *Ramayana* and various Puranas were transcribed. The development of the Pali canon, associated with early Buddhist texts, also played a significant role in the spread of the written culture.

The medieval period saw the rise of regional languages and literature, with significant works produced in Tamil, Kannada, Telugu, Marathi and Bengali. Manuscript culture thrived, and many texts were copied and preserved by Jain, Buddhist and Hindu scholars. The establishment of libraries in temples and educational institutions facilitated the preservation and dissemination of knowledge.

The Mughal era (1526–1857) introduced Persian and Arabic literary traditions into India. The Mughal emperors were patrons of the arts and literature and the establishment of scriptoriums (maktabs) and the use of paper, which was brought in from China, contributed to the spread of written texts. This period also saw the creation of illustrated manuscripts and miniature paintings.

The entry of Europeans and especially British colonialism changed the Indian publishing scene significantly. The introduction of the printing press in India by Jesuit missionaries in the mid-16th century revolutionized the production of books. The first printing press in India was established in Goa in 1556.

In the 19th century, printing technology advanced, and several presses were established in major cities like Calcutta (now Kolkata), Bombay (now Mumbai) and Madras (now Chennai). The Serampore Mission Press, established by William Carey and his colleagues in 1800, is of special importance as it printed religious texts, dictionaries and educational materials in various Indian languages.

After independence in 1947, India's publishing industry experienced significant growth. The government established institutions like the National Book Trust (NBT) in 1957 and the Sahitya Akademi to promote literature and publishing. Indian authors began gaining international recognition, and the country's rich literary tradition continued to flourish.

Today, India is one of the largest producers of books in the world, publishing in numerous languages and catering to a diverse readership. The Indian publishing industry encompasses a wide range of genres, including academic, literary, educational and popular fiction and non-fiction. The rise of digital publishing and e-books has further expanded access to literature.

THE HISTORY OF BOOKS AND PUBLISHING IN INDIA TESTIFIES TO THE COUNTRY'S ONGOING COMMITMENT TO THE DISSEMINATION OF KNOWLEDGE.

All this means that readers have to adapt to the changing reading formats and for this, they need to embrace the diverse ways in which information is presented and consumed in today's digital age. Here are some strategies to effectively navigate and enjoy different reading formats.

1 Explore Different Ways of 'Reading'

While audiobooks might be new, telling stories isn't. In fact, oral literature is where it all started. So be open to different ways of exploring narratives, and don't see it from an angle of something being 'lost' in these new-fangled formats.

2 Use eReaders and Apps

Invest in an eReader or use reading apps on your devices. These tools often provide customizable settings for font size, background colour, and other features to enhance your reading experience.

3 Try Audiobook Platforms

Explore audiobook platforms that offer a wide range of titles narrated by skilled performers and narrators. A popular example is Stephen Fry's reading of the Harry Potter books. Audiobooks can be a great option for multitasking, such as listening during commutes or workouts or even when dusting your house.

4 Combine Print and Digital

Consider integrating both print and digital formats into your reading routine. For some, certain genres or situations may be more conducive to print, while others are better suited for digital formats.

5 Adapt to Screen Reading

If you find yourself reading more content on screens, practice healthy screen reading habits. Adjust screen brightness, use blue light filters, and take breaks to avoid eye strain.

6 Join Online Book Communities

Engage with online book communities on platforms like Goodreads or social media. These communities often discuss a variety of reading formats, offering recommendations and insights into different genres and styles.

7 Adopt Flexible Reading Habits

Be open to adapting your reading habits based on the content and context. For instance, reserve print books for quiet evenings at home, while using audiobooks when on the metro or travelling.

8 Embrace Multimedia

Explore multimedia content that combines text with images, audio and video. Platforms like interactive eBooks, educational apps, and digital magazines offer engaging and dynamic reading experiences.

9 Stay Informed about Publishing Trends

Stay informed about emerging publishing trends, such as interactive eBooks, virtual reality literature, and other innovative formats. This knowledge can broaden your reading choices.

10 Utilize Library Resources

Take advantage of digital resources provided by libraries, such as eBook lending platforms and audiobook services. Many libraries offer a variety of digital materials to members.

11 Be Open to Experimentation

Experiment with different formats and platforms to find what works best for you. Personal preferences may vary, and adapting to changing reading formats often involves a degree of experimentation.

Some popular online reading communities:

1 Goodreads

Goodreads is one of the largest and most well-known online reading communities. Users can create virtual bookshelves, track their reading progress, write reviews, join book clubs and participate in reading challenges. Goodreads is a platform owned by Amazon.

2 LibraryThing

LibraryThing is a social cataloguing website that allows users to catalogue their personal libraries, write reviews and connect with other readers. It features discussion forums, book recommendations and various book-related features.

3 Bookish

Bookish is an online platform that offers book recommendations, author interviews and articles about literature. Users can join discussions, participate in reading challenges and discover new books based on their preferences.

4 Reddit Book Communities

Reddit has numerous book-related communities (subreddits) where readers can discuss specific genres, share book recommendations and participate in book-related discussions. Examples include r/books, r/Fantasy and r/ScienceFiction.

5 Instagram Bookstagram Community

Bookstagram is a community on Instagram where users share photos of books, write reviews and engage in book-related discussions using the hashtag #bookstagram. Many bookstagrammers create visually appealing book-related content.

6 Litsy

Litsy is a social media platform designed specifically for booklovers. Users can post book reviews, share quotes and participate in themed challenges. The platform combines elements of social media and book blogging.

7 Shelfari

Shelfari is an online book club and community owned by Amazon. Users can create virtual bookshelves, write reviews and connect with other readers. Shelfari shares some features with Goodreads.

8 Book Riot

Book Riot offers book-related content, including articles, podcasts and book recommendations. Readers can engage in discussions and explore diverse book genres.

9 The StoryGraph

The StoryGraph is a platform that helps readers track their reading, discover new books and connect with fellow readers. It offers personalized book recommendations based on individual preferences.

10 Sonali's Book Club

Reading has always been something I loved, but over time, I felt a disconnect with books amid the hustle and bustle of life. That's when this club was born – to inspire me to return to reading and to explore books with people from all over the world.

These online reading communities cater to a variety of tastes and preferences, providing readers with opportunities to connect with others who share their love for books and literature. Whether you're seeking book recommendations, participating in discussions or tracking your reading progress, these platforms offer diverse ways to engage with the world of books.

AND MORE!

A pictorial script, often referred to as a logographic script, is a writing system in which characters or symbols represent words, morphemes or semantic units. Instead of using an alphabet where each symbol represents a sound (as in English), pictorial scripts use symbols or characters that directly convey meaning.

Pictorial scripts are visually rich and often require a significant number of characters to represent the full range of meanings in a language. Learning such scripts typically involves memorizing a large number of symbols and their associated meanings, making them complex but expressive systems of communication. While some pictorial scripts have ancient origins, others continue to be used in modern times alongside other writing systems. For instance, Mandarin. Logograms are used in the writing systems of China, Japan, South and North Korea and other East Asian countries.

Kanji is a system of logographic characters used in the modern Japanese writing system. Many kanji characters were adopted from Chinese characters, although some have unique meanings in Japanese.

Ancient Egyptian hieroglyphs were a complex system of logographic and alphabetic elements. The ancient Mayan civilization used a script consisting of logograms and syllabic symbols. Mayan glyphs were carved into stone monuments and codices and were employed for recording historical events and religious texts.

Sumerian cuneiform is one of the earliest known writing systems and features a combination of logograms and syllabic elements. It was used in ancient Mesopotamia. The Aztecs of Mesoamerica had a system of pictorial writing that combined logograms, syllabic elements, and phonetic signs.

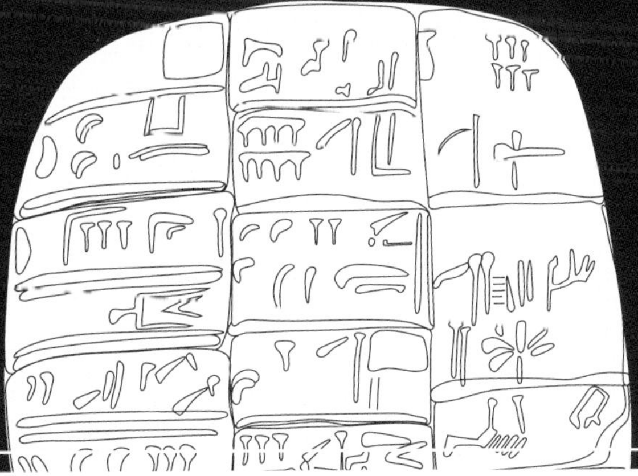

HOW AND WHERE I READ

My reading corner

My preferred format to read

My favourite time of the day to read

Why I like to read a book

Other formats I've tried – Ebooks

Audio books

5

BOOK ENCHANTED

Starting Young

It is never too early to give a child a start in reading. In fact, some even feel that reading to the foetus is beneficial to the baby. So how do you help children become readers? By reading with them, by telling them stories, and by making books a part of daily life.

All the things that you usually do with children – singing songs, teaching them rhymes, listening to their stories, asking them to draw pictures related to stories – all contribute towards helping them grow into readers and booklovers. Playing developmentally appropriate games such as alliteration games, oral blending, alphabet recognition, letter sounds and word games all help children learn to read and develop a love for books.

Science has shown that reading is as important as touching, talking and smiling in the growth of a child's brain, especially in the first few years. So, it is never too early to start reading with children. Reading can become a habit, almost like obedience, the gift that Ella gets from the fairy Lucinda.

These things can help turn pre-schoolers into readers.

1. **Create reading rituals.** Assign a particular time to reading and do it every day. With pre-schoolers, opt for books with colourful pictures that can help stimulate their mind and their imagination.

2. **Read with expression, emphasizing on rhyme and rhythm.** Use different voices for characters. Pre-schoolers love it. Roar like a lion, whine like a chipmunk, mew like a cat and growl like a grinch. You will have the child asking for more every day.

3. **Visit the library with your pre-schooler.** Regular trips to the library expose pre-schoolers to a variety of books and foster a love for reading. Encourage participation in the activities there such as storytelling sessions, book-reading and writing.

4 **Make reading an interactive activity.** Encourage preschoolers to engage with the story by asking questions, making predictions and discussing the illustrations. This enhances their comprehension and critical thinking skills.

5 **Promote writing and creativity.** Encourage children to express themselves through writing, drawing and painting inspired by the stories they've read. You can also incorporate puzzles related to their favourite books to reinforce story comprehension.

6 **Lead by example.** Serve as a positive role model by demonstrating your own enjoyment of reading and discussing books with enthusiasm. Your enthusiasm for reading will inspire them to view reading as an enjoyable activity worth pursuing.

When it comes to kindergarten kids, many of these will still work but you need to tweak the list a bit. Here are some ideas.

1. Introduce read-aloud books for a slightly older child. Make reading aloud a daily activity. This will not only improve their vocabulary, but they will also learn to modulate the voice and read with expression.

2. Library visits should be more frequent and regular for this age group. You can also borrow eBooks but ensure that physical books are a major part of their life. Children will use screens, but the tactile nature of books is good for focus and also to learn the joy of reading a physical book with illustrations.

3. Get children of this age to create their own stories and narrate them to you and to their peers. They could also narrate stories they have read in books. This will enhance their enjoyment of books and they will remember more of what they read.

READING ALOUD STIMULATES CHILDREN'S IMAGINATION AND DEVELOPS AN INTEREST IN BOOKS THAT WILL STAY WITH THEM FOR LIFE.

Reading aloud to and with young children not only promotes language learning, but it also correlates with the development of literacy, comprehension and later academic success. Reading aloud stimulates children's imagination and develops an interest in books that will stay with them for life. It improves their listening skills and builds their vocabulary.

Research shows that five key elements of reading among children contribute to the development of strong literacy skills.

1 Phonemic Awareness

Phonemic awareness is the ability to recognize and manipulate individual sounds (phonemes) in spoken words. Children with strong phonemic awareness can identify rhymes, segment words into individual sounds, and blend sounds to form words. Activities like rhyming games and phonemic awareness exercises help develop this crucial skill.

This will help them appreciate, for example, Lewis Carroll's poetry which is marked by the same clever word play and imagination as seen in *Alice's Adventures in Wonderland* and *Through the Looking Glass*. Children love his poems such as *Jabberwocky* from *Through the Looking Glass* as well as his last poem *The Hunting of the Snark* which has an extremely promising beginning.

"Just the place for a Snark!"
the Bellman cried,
As he landed his crew with care;
Supporting each man on the top of the tide
By a finger entwined in his hair.

"Just the place for a Snark! I have said it twice:
That alone should encourage the crew.
Just the place for a Snark! I have said it thrice:
What I tell you three times is true."

Similarly, children will enjoy the nonsense rhymes of Sukumar Ray, father of eminent filmmaker Satyajit Ray. *The Sons of Ramgaroo* is fun as seen in the opening lines itself:

To the sons of Ramgaroo

Laughter is taboo

A funny tale will make them wail:

"We're not amused, boo – hoo!"

2 Phonics

Phonics involves understanding the relationship between letters and their sounds. Children learn to decode words by associating letters with their corresponding sounds. Phonics helps children become fluent readers and spellers. It includes activities like letter-sound correspondence, blending sounds and recognizing sight words.

3 Vocabulary Development

Vocabulary development is essential for comprehension. Children need to build a robust vocabulary to understand and express themselves effectively. Reading a variety of books, engaging in conversations and exposure to a diverse range of words in different contexts contribute to vocabulary growth.

In Lucy M. Montgomery's *Anne of Green Gables*, Anne decides to learn one big word every day because as she says, "if you have big ideas, you have to use big words to express them, haven't you?"

4 Reading Fluency

Fluency is the ability to read accurately, smoothly and with expression. Fluent readers can decode words effortlessly, allowing them to focus on comprehension. Reading regularly and practicing with texts at an appropriate difficulty level contribute to the development of reading fluency.

tableau demure bequeath

ingenuous wistful

5 Comprehension Skills

Comprehension is the ultimate goal of reading. Children need to understand the meaning of the text, make connections, infer and analyze information. Comprehension skills involve asking questions, summarizing, predicting and actively engaging with the material. Teachers and parents can support comprehension by discussing stories, asking open-ended questions and encouraging critical thinking.

These elements are interconnected, and effective reading instruction often integrates various strategies to address each aspect. Additionally, fostering a positive attitude towards reading, providing an environment rich in books and encouraging a love of books are overarching principles that contribute to a child's overall reading development.

EACH CHiLD iS UNiQUE, AND EDUCATORS AND PARENTS SHOULD TAiLOR THEiR APPROACH TO MEET THE iNDiViDUAL NEEDS AND iNTERESTS OF EACH LEARNER.

Fairytales can spark an interest in children who are not readers and turn them into booklovers. The enduring popularity of fairytales attests to the fact that they can attract readers and non-readers because of their intrinsic story value.

Just as *Ella Enchanted* is a retelling of the story of Cinderella but also so much richer for the way it is written and for the introduction of various characters. Fairytales also teach children valuable lessons in humanity and culture without being didactic. Also, as many of them came down via the oral tradition, they contain a genetic memory of sorts that also makes them rich and valuable.

The other day, visiting a Christmas fete, I noticed the biggest crowd at the stall selling stationery and books. Each child had a book in hand. Similar scenes can be seen at bookshops and book fairs. Given a chance, children will choose their books. So, it is a great idea to let them build a personal library. Let them start small and they can even earn money by doing odd jobs which can be spent on buying books. The excitement on children's faces when they get a new book is more than enough for any parent if any justification was needed.

Building a child's personal library is a wonderful way to foster a love of reading and provide a rich learning environment.

Here are some tips to help you build a diverse and engaging collection.

1 Start Early

Begin building your child's library from an early age. Infants and toddlers benefit from board books with simple illustrations and tactile features.

2 Include Classics

Incorporate classic children's books that have stood the test of time. Classics provide timeless stories and illustrations that resonate across generations. Apart from the books already mentioned such as the *Anne of Green Gables* series and Enid Blyton's, you can include the Katy Did books, R.L. Stevenson, Daniel Defoe's *Robinson Crusoe* and the Mary Poppins series by P. L. Travers.

3 Explore Various Genres

Include a variety of genres to cater to different interests. This may include picture books, early readers, chapter books, fairytales, folktales, poetry and non-fiction.

4 Consider Diversity

Prioritize diversity in your child's collection, including books that feature characters from various backgrounds, cultures and experiences. A diverse library helps children develop empathy and an understanding of the world around them.

5 Choose Quality Books

Select books with engaging stories, beautiful illustrations and age-appropriate content. Look for award-winning books and those recommended by educators and literacy experts.

6 Build a Series Collection

Children love book series that follow the adventures of beloved characters. They can encourage children to read more and become invested in the characters' journeys. The Harry Potter and Lemony Snicket books are good examples of bestselling series.

7 Include Interactive Books

Incorporate interactive books, such as lift-the-flap books, pop-up books and books with texture. Interactive elements can enhance the reading experience and make it more enjoyable for young readers.

8 Follow the Child's Interests

Pay attention to your child's interests and include books related to his or her hobbies, favourite animals and activities. This personalization will make the library more engaging for the child.

9 Visit Bookstores and Libraries

Regularly visit bookshops and libraries to discover new releases and explore different genres. Allow your child to choose books based on his or her preferences.

10 Create a Cozy Reading Nook

Designate a cozy reading nook in your home where your child can enjoy reading comfortably. Include soft pillows, blankets and proper lighting to make the space inviting.

11 Rotate Books

Periodically rotate the books in your child's library to keep the collection fresh and maintain their interest. This is especially beneficial for younger children who enjoy revisiting familiar stories.

12 Gift Books

Encourage family and friends to gift the child books for birthdays, holidays or special occasions. Building a library can be a collaborative effort that involves the whole community.

REMEMBER THAT BUILDING A CHILDREN'S LIBRARY IS A GRADUAL PROCESS, AND THE GOAL IS TO CREATE A NURTURING ENVIRONMENT THAT ENCOURAGES A LIFELONG LOVE OF READING.

As your child grows, the library can evolve to meet changing interests and reading levels.

AND MORE!

The Bologna Children's Book Fair is the biggest in the publishing industry and brings together a unique and diverse global audience to Bologna, Italy. And it has been doing this for 60 years. It is the world's premium copyright exchange hub when it comes to publishing that extends to current multimedia and licensing businesses for children's stories, illustration, animation and related areas.

Publishers, illustrators, graphic designers, literary agents, authors, translators, mobile developers, licensors and licensees, packagers, printers, distributors, audiobook professionals, booksellers, brands, librarians and teachers all flock to the event each spring to experience the world of books and multimedia products in hundreds of booths across six huge halls.

The famous Illustrators Exhibition and industry recognized BolognaRagazzi awards make this event so special.

The fair is a unique mix of a cultural book show and an international rights business forum for all types of content for children. BolognaBookPlus, the brand extension dedicated to general trade publishing organized in co-operation with AIE (Italian Publishers Association) and Bologna Licensing Trade Fair/Kids, has become an integral part of Bologna Children's Book Fair. It brings major international licensing and entertainment players together.

At the fair, the International Board on Books for Young People (IBBY) announces the Hans Christian Andersen Award, the highest international recognition given to an author and an illustrator of children's books. Given every other year by IBBY, the Hans Christian Andersen Awards recognize lifelong achievement and are presented to those whose complete works have made an important, lasting contribution in the field of children's literature.

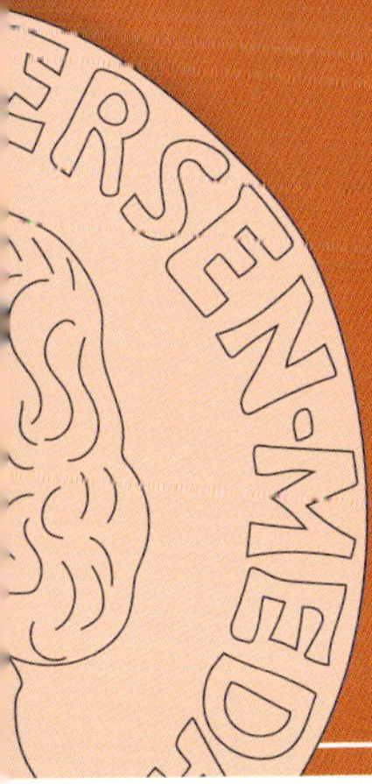

CREATE YOUR OWN STORY!

The beginning

The middle

The end

Fill in the story & details of the characters

Add sketches

6
GOLDEN TICKET
ONE HUNDRED YEARS OF READiNG
Book Recommendations

Ever since writing was invented and the codex format was created, to today where books are part and parcel of our existence, the written word has been the most powerful in driving history, spreading religion, shaping cultures and preserving knowledge.

The journey of the written word, from ancient scrolls to modern e-books, reflects the evolution of human communication and the profound impact of literature on our collective consciousness. Throughout history, books have been instrumental in disseminating ideas, fostering intellectual growth and connecting people across time and space. Religious texts, such as the Bible, the Quran and the Vedas, have shaped the beliefs and practices of billions, guiding civilizations and influencing moral frameworks.

The written word has been a catalyst for revolutions and social movements, from the Enlightenment's philosophical treatises to the influential writings of people like Martin Luther King Jr. and Mahatma Gandhi. Books have sparked imagination, challenged norms and inspired individuals to question authority.

Literature has been a powerful tool in the preservation of cultural heritage.

THE WRITTEN WORD HAS IMMORTALIZED THE THOUGHTS OF POETS, PHILOSOPHERS AND THINKERS, PROVIDING A TIMELESS RECORD OF HUMAN ACHIEVEMENTS, STRUGGLES AND ASPIRATIONS.

Epic poems, ancient manuscripts and classical works have carried the stories and wisdom of civilizations from one generation to the next.

In today's digital age, books continue to play a central role in shaping our understanding of the world. Online platforms, e-books and audiobooks have expanded access to information, fostering global conversations and connecting diverse communities. As we navigate the ever-changing landscape of literature, books remain a beacon of enlightenment, a source of solace and a catalyst for progress. Books continue to be the threads that weave the fabric of our shared human experience, transcending borders, languages and time periods.

BOOKS PROVIDE SOMETHING FOR EVERYONE. AS J.K. ROWLING, AUTHOR OF THE HARRY POTTER BOOKS SAID, "IF YOU DON'T LIKE TO READ, YOU HAVEN'T FOUND THE RIGHT BOOK."

But the book is there, it has been written.
You just have to find it. And it is a guarantee,
that you will be a fan forever of books,
the written word.

The Top 10: The Greatest Books of All Time

100 of the Best Books of All Time

The top 10 books to read in your lifetime

There are innumerable lists floating around of books that are considered must-reads. They are all good but rather than trying to follow a list, follow your heart. Pick up the book that you want to read, not what someone else wants you to read. That being said, here is a list of the top ten picture books, children's books and adults' books that can help start you off. However, this comes with the disclaimer that this is neither the final word nor an infallible list. So, feel free to come up with your own list of must-read books using these lists as just a guidance.

Picture Books That You Need to Read

1 The Little Match Girl

This story by Hans Christian Andersen published in 1845 is one of his most famous and poignant tales, often classified as a literary fairytale. The story follows a poor little girl who is forced to sell matches on New Year's Eve.

The story urges readers to reflect on the importance of empathy and kindness towards those who are less fortunate. Andersen's *The Little Match Girl* has been adapted into various forms of media, including ballets, operas and animated films. Its enduring appeal lies in its ability to evoke deep emotions and provoke contemplation about social justice and the human condition.

2 Goodnight Moon

A classic children's book written by Margaret Wise Brown and illustrated by Clement Hurd, it was first published in 1947 and has since become a beloved bedtime story for generations of children.

The story follows a young rabbit saying goodnight to everything around, both animate and inanimate, in its room such as the moon, the stars, a red balloon, a quiet old lady whispering "hush" and many more. The list gradually winds down, creating a sense of closure and tranquillity.

3 The Giving Tree

Written and illustrated by Shel Silverstein, the book was first published in 1964 and has become one of his most well-known and widely read works.

The story revolves around the relationship between a boy and a tree. The narrative unfolds in a series of episodes as the boy grows from childhood to old age. The tree, which loves the boy unconditionally, provides him with various gifts at different stages of his life. In his youth, the boy enjoys playing in the tree's branches and eating its apples. As he grows older, he seeks different things from the tree.

Despite the boy's increasing demands and the tree's sacrifices, it remains devoted to him. In the end, when the boy is old and tired, he returns to the tree. The tree, now reduced to a stump, expresses joy that it can offer the boy a place to sit and rest.

4 The Lorax

A book written by the prolific author for children, Theodor Seuss Geisel, or Dr Seuss as he is commonly known, *The Lorax* was first published in 1971. It is a classic work of environmental literature with a strong message on the importance of conservation. The story is known for its whimsical characters, rhyming language and vibrant illustrations.

The Lorax has been adapted into various media, including an animated television special in 1972 and a feature film in 2012. It remains a widely read and discussed book, and its themes continue to resonate with readers.

5 A Bear Called Paddington

A children's book by Michael Bond, it was first published in 1958. The book introduces the character of Paddington Bear, a friendly and polite bear from Peru who travels to London and is adopted by the Brown family.

Throughout the stories, Paddington's innocence, good intentions and mishaps result in humorous and heart-warming moments. He often misunderstands aspects of British culture, leading to comical situations and lovable moments of cultural exchange.

A Bear Called Paddington is the first book in the series featuring Paddington Bear. Bond went on to write numerous Paddington books, and the character became a beloved icon in children's literature. The series has been translated into multiple languages and adapted into various forms of media, including animated television series and a feature film.

6 Winnie-the-Pooh

Another classic children's book series created by author A.A. Milne who based the protagonist on his son, Christopher Robin's favourite stuffed bear. The stories feature the adventures of Winnie-the-Pooh, a lovable and slightly dim-witted bear, and his friends, including Christopher Robin, in the Hundred Acre Wood. The series has become a beloved part of children's literature and has been adapted into various media.

7 Eloise

The first of the Eloise series of books was published in 1955. Written by Kay Thompson and illustrated by Hilary Knight, it is a classic children's book because of its charming and whimsical storytelling. And, of course, because of the distinctive character of Eloise.

Eloise is a precocious and imaginative 6-year-old girl who lives at the luxury hotel, The Plaza, in New York City with her British nanny, her pug dog Weenie and her turtle Skipperdee. Eloise's adventures often involve exploring the hotel, interacting with its staff and creating chaos in a charming and endearing way.

The charm of Eloise's adventures continues to captivate new generations of readers, and The Plaza Hotel itself has embraced the character's legacy, offering themed Eloise suites and events.

8 Love You Forever

A children's book written by Canadian author Robert Munsch and illustrated by Sheila McGraw that was first published in 1986 and has since become a classic.

The story revolves around the relationship between a mother and her baby son.

Its heartfelt message about the enduring nature of parental love has made it a popular choice for bedtime reading.

9 The Gruffalo

The Gruffalo is a popular children's book written by Julia Donaldson and illustrated by Axel Scheffler. First published in 1999, the book tells the story of a clever mouse who takes a stroll through the deep, dark woods. To avoid being eaten by various predators, the mouse invents a creature called the Gruffalo—a monstrous creature with terrible features.

10 The Very Hungry Caterpillar

Written and illustrated by Eric Carle, *The Very Hungry Caterpillar* was first published in 1969.

The story follows the journey of a tiny egg on a leaf, which eventually hatches into a very hungry caterpillar. The caterpillar begins its week-long eating spree, consuming a variety of foods each day. It starts with one apple on Monday, two pears on Tuesday, three plums on Wednesday, and so on.

The book's distinctive collage-style illustrations and the rhythmic and repetitive text have made it a favourite. *The Very Hungry Caterpillar* is often used in educational settings to teach basic concepts, and its timeless appeal continues to captivate new generations of readers.

11 The Tiger Who Came to Tea

Published in 1968, Judith Kerr's *The Tiger Who Came to Tea* is a children's story that has stood the test of time. Sophie is having tea with her mother in the kitchen when the doorbell rings. She opens the door to see a big, furry, stripey tiger.

Kerr described the tale as a tale she made up for her little daughter. She loved visiting the zoo with her daughter Tacy, and particularly liked looking at the "beautiful" tigers. "It was just a bedtime story I made up for my daughter when she was two, getting on for three. I knew it by heart, every word. It hadn't changed because you watch your child's face and obviously you leave out bits gradually if they look bored. I told it to her again and again and again, and she used to say, 'Talk the tiger'. When I decided to do the book, I remember wondering what the tiger should look like, whether he should have clothes," she said.

12 Where the Wild Things Are

Written by Maurice Sendak, *Where the Wild Things Are* tells the story of a young boy named Max who is sent to his room without supper as punishment for wearing a wolf's suit and misbehaving. There he imagines a fantastical journey where his bedroom becomes an island inhabited by wild creatures. Max tames the wild things and becomes their king, leading them in a series of wild adventures. It celebrates the wildness and creativity of childhood while also acknowledging the need for love and security. Most of all, it deals with the comfort and familiarity of home.

13 Wave

This picture book by Suzy Lee captures a child's wonder and joy at the beach. The illustrations convey the wonder of the ocean and the child's imagination beautifully.

14 Amar Chitra Katha series

I am including this in picture books as they are illustrated in the comic-book style. But the stories could easily place these books in the children's books list. The brainchild of Anant Pai, lovingly called Uncle Pai, Amar Chitra Katha is a popular comic book series that retells traditional Indian stories, mythology and folklore in a visually engaging format. He began the series in 1967 to teach Indian children about their culture and heritage. Amar Chitra Katha has since become an integral part of Indian popular culture.

15 Wabi Sabi

This beautifully illustrated book by Mark Reibstein introduces the complex Japanese philosophy of Wabi Sabi or appreciating the transient nature of everything and accepting imperfections. It is a great children's book that is invaluable for adults too.

Children's Books That You Need to Read

1 Little Women

Louisa May Alcott's book deals with the lives of four sisters – Meg, Jo, Beth and Amy – loosely based on her own life and that of her sisters. Set against the background of the American Civil War, the book was a huge success when it was published in two volumes in 1868 and 1869 and has since become one of the most beloved and enduring works of children's literature. Often categorized as a coming-of-age novel, it is known for its exploration of family, love, and the pursuit of personal aspirations.

Little Women has left an indelible mark on literature and popular culture. It continues to be celebrated for its portrayal of familial bonds and the pursuit of one's dreams, making it a classic that transcends generations.

2 The Borrowers

A children's fantasy novel written by Mary Norton, *The Borrowers* was published in 1952 and is the first in a series of novels featuring the tiny people known as Borrowers.

The Borrowers has been widely acclaimed for its imaginative storytelling and charming depiction of the miniature world inhabited by the Borrowers. Norton's writing style and the delightful illustrations by Diana Stanley contribute to the book's appeal.

The Borrowers was followed by *The Borrowers Afield* (1955), *The Borrowers Afloat* (1959) and *The Borrowers Aloft* (1961).

The Borrowers' theme of resourcefulness and resilience in the face of adversity has resonated with children, making it a classic that continues to captivate new generations.

3 Anne of Green Gables

Anne of Green Gables, written by Canadian author Lucy Maud Montgomery, better known as L.M. Montgomery, introduces the lovable heroine, Anne Shirley. The book was first published in 1908 and has since become one of the most beloved works of children's literature.

Set in the late 19th century on Canada's Prince Edward Island, the book follows the adventures and misadventures of Anne, an imaginative and spirited orphan girl.

Anne of Green Gables has become a children's classic and is one of Canada's most famous literary works.

The success of the first book led to a series of sequels, including *Anne of Avonlea*, *Anne of the Island* and several others that follow Anne's life and adventures as she grows into adulthood.

The GRINCH

4 How the Grinch Stole Christmas!

A holiday classic children's book written and illustrated by Dr. Seuss, *How the Grinch Stole Christmas!* was first published in 1957 and has since become one of the most beloved and enduring Christmas stories.

How the Grinch Stole Christmas! emphasizes that Christmas is about more than just material possessions – it is about the joy of togetherness and the warmth of the holiday spirit.

The character of the Grinch and the message of kindness and generosity have made the story an enduring classic, and it continues to be a favourite during the Christmas season. The phrase **"You're a mean one, Mr. Grinch"** and the Grinch's eventual change of heart have become iconic elements of the holiday tradition.

5 A Christmas Carol

A Christmas Carol is a novella written by famous British author Charles Dickens that was first published in 1843.

The novella tells the story of Ebenezer Scrooge, a miserly and cold-hearted old man who despises Christmas and everything associated with it.

A Christmas Carol deals with the idea of redemption, compassion and the transformative power of love and generosity.
It serves as a powerful reminder of the importance of empathy and kindness, especially during the holiday season. The character of Ebenezer Scrooge has become an iconic figure, and the phrase "**Bah, humbug!**" is often associated with his miserly attitude.

6 The Harry Potter series

This blockbuster series by J.K. Rowling consists of seven fantasy novels that centre around the life of Harry Potter, a young wizard studying at the Hogwarts School of Witchcraft and Wizadry, along with his friends Hermoine Granger and Ron Weasley.

The Harry Potter series has become a global phenomenon, with millions of copies sold and translations into numerous languages. The books have been adapted into a successful film series, and the world of Harry Potter has expanded to include spin-off works, theme park attractions and more.

7 Stories From the Panchatantra

The Panchatantra is an ancient Indian collection of animal fables and moral stories, primarily written in Sanskrit. The word Panchatantra is derived from two Sanskrit words, Pancha meaning five, and Tantra, meaning principles or strategies.

The Panchatantra is traditionally attributed to the ancient Indian scholar and teacher Vishnu Sharma. According to legend, the stories were composed to teach three young princes how to become good rulers.

The collection is organized into five books, each dealing with different aspects of worldly

> **THE PRIMARY PURPOSE OF *THE PANCHATANTRA* IS TO IMPART MORAL VALUES, STRATEGIES FOR SUCCESS, AND PRACTICAL WISDOM.**

wisdom and moral conduct through the means of animal fables. *The Panchatantra* features a variety of animal characters, each representing different human traits and characteristics. Lions, monkeys, birds and other creatures act out human-like situations and dilemmas. The primary purpose of *The Panchatantra* is to impart moral values, strategies for success and practical wisdom.

The Panchatantra is considered one of the earliest examples of animal fables and has had a significant influence on world literature. Its stories have been translated into numerous languages and have inspired similar collections, including Aesop's Fables.

8 Heidi

Written by Swiss author Johanna Spyri, *Heidi* has charmed generations of children. Originally published in two parts in 1880 and 1881, the novel has become one of the best-known works of children's literature.

Heidi tells the story of a young, orphaned girl named Heidi who is initially raised by her aunt Dete. However, due to Dete's need to take up a job in Frankfurt, Heidi is sent to live with her reclusive and gruff grandfather, Alpöhi (Alm-Uncle), in a small hut high in the Alps.

Heidi's story continues to be popular. The novel explores the themes of nature, family, friendship and the healing power of nature. Its enduring popularity is a testament to Johanna Spyri's storytelling and the universal themes of love, resilience and the beauty of the natural world.

9 The Lion, the Witch and the Wardrobe

The Chronicles of Narnia is a series of seven fantasy novels written by British author C.S. Lewis, the first of which is *The Lion, the Witch and the Wardrobe*. The books, written between 1949 and 1954, have been immensely popular and have been adapted into various films, TV series and stage productions.

The novel explores themes of courage, sacrifice, betrayal and the triumph of good over evil. It is a Christian allegory, and each of the Pevensie siblings plays a unique role in the unfolding events, with Aslan guiding and supporting them. Aslan the lion represents Christ, embodying sacrifice and redemption through his death and resurrection, while the White Witch symbolizes temptation and evil.

The Lion, the Witch and the Wardrobe captivates children with its magical world and compelling characters. The novel's enduring popularity lies in its rich storytelling, imaginative world-building and the timeless themes it explores.

10 The Chalet School in Exile

Part of the Chalet School series of books belonging to the school story genre, *The Chalet School in Exile* was published in 1940. Written by the prolific author Elinor M. Brent-Dyer, the series comprises 58 books. This book, which is the most exciting of the series, is set against the background of World War II. The Chalet School, which was begun in the Austrian Tyrol by Madge with just two students – her sister Jo and a neighbour's child, Grizel – had grown to become a well-known and big school when it is forced to move from its location due to the threat of the Nazis. The school relocates to a temporary home in Guernsey, an island in the English Channel. The story deals with the challenges faced by the school community as they adapt to their new surroundings and navigate the impact of the war.

The novel explores themes of resilience, friendship and the impact of war on a close-knit community. Despite the challenges, the characters in the Chalet School series demonstrate strength and solidarity as they continue their educational pursuits in exile.

11 Charlie and the Chocolate Factory

One of Roald Dahl's most popular children's books, *Charlie and the Chocolate Factory,* follows the adventures of a young boy named Charlie Bucket, who belongs to a poor family and lives in a small house with his parents and four grandparents. Written in 1964, the tale begins with the eccentric chocolatier, Willy Wonka, announcing a worldwide contest where five golden tickets are hidden in his chocolate bars. These golden tickets grant the winners a tour of his mysterious and magical chocolate factory.

Charlie's life changes when he finds the last golden ticket. *Charlie and the Chocolate Factory* is a timeless tale of imagination, morality and the power of kindness, captivating readers of all ages with its whimsical storytelling and memorable characters.

12 Wonder

Published in 2012, ***Wonder*** tells the story of August Pullman, a young boy born with a facial deformity that has led to him being home-schooled. The novel follows August as he enters fifth grade at Beecher Prep School, marking his first experience in a traditional school setting. R.J. Palacio is said to have been inspired to write the book after his daughter broke into tears on seeing a schoolmate with a facial deformity.

Narrated from multiple perspectives – August's, his sister Via's, and those of his classmates – the novel explores the themes of bullying, friendship, acceptance and empathy. August faces various challenges and prejudices due to his appearance but also finds support from his classmates like Jack Will and Summer.

A heart-warming and inspirational tale that resonates with readers of all ages, *Wonder* encourages empathy and understanding for those who are different. It emphasizes the importance of kindness and acceptance in creating a more inclusive and compassionate world.

13 The Book Thief

Written by Australian author Markus Zusak, *The Book Thief* is set in Nazi Germany during World War II. The narrator of the story is Death, who has found the book written by an old woman Liesel Meminger when she was a young girl in Germany.

The Book Thief is a moving and thought-provoking book that explores themes of friendship, loss and the human capacity for both cruelty and compassion. It highlights the importance of literature in preserving humanity and finding beauty in the midst of tragedy.

14 Matilda

This book by Roald Dahl is an evergreen bestseller. Matilda's efforts to best a cruel headmistress is a wonderful tale of empowerment and the triumph of good over evil.

15 Enid Blyton's Nature Lover's Book

This book has stood the test of time. Published in 1944, it has gone into numerous reprints and is still as loved today as when it first came out. With naturalist Uncle Merry introducing the wonders of nature in every season to three children, the book is non-fiction made attractive through fiction. Its message of conservation is even more relevant in today's world which is being threatened by climate change and environmental destruction.

16 Percy Jackson

The Percy Jackson series of books by Rick Riordan is popular with children because they are able to relate to the protagonist on various levels. His unique abilities because of being half-god with Poseidon for a father blend well with the time-honoured themes of loyalty and friendship, heroism and sacrifice.

Top Classics that you Need to Read

1 Murder on the Orient Express

One of mystery-and-crime author Agatha Christie's best novels, it was first published in 1934. The novel features the Belgian detective Hercule Poirot and is known for its intricate plot and clever resolution.

Christie's meticulous storytelling and the memorable character of Hercule Poirot have contributed to the enduring popularity of the novel. It is often cited as one of the greatest mystery novels ever written.

2 The Great Gatsby

F. Scott Fitzgerald's iconic novel was first published in 1925 and has since become one of the greatest American classics. The novel is set in the summer of 1922 and explores the themes of wealth, love, decadence and most of all, the American Dream.

The Great Gatsby is considered by many as one of the greatest novels ever written. While it initially received mixed reviews and had moderate success during Fitzgerald's lifetime, it gained immense popularity in the decades following his death. The character of Jay Gatsby and the themes explored in the novel continue to resonate with readers and scholars alike.

3 Pride and Prejudice

Written by Jane Austen and published in 1813, *Pride and Prejudice* has one of the most famous opening lines in English literature: "It is a truth universally acknowledged, that a single man in possession of a good fortune, must be in want of a wife." It brilliantly posits the theme of the novel and the most important idea in 19th century Britain when women had few choices, especially if they did not have a fortune or a man to look after them. It is today one of the most beloved and widely read novels. The novel is full of witty social commentary, memorable characters and is a biting study of class and society in Regency England.

4 The Return of the Native

Thomas Hardy's late 19th century novel is a study of the mores and morals of Victorian England, especially rural England. *The Return of the Native* carries forward his idea of a universe ruled by an indifferent power that is uncaring about moral justice or consequences. Wessex, the region of England that is associated with Hardy's novels, is where he was brought up and in the novel the region, represented by Egdon Heath, is almost a character.

5 Alias Grace

Alias Grace is a historical novel written by Canadian author Margaret Atwood that was published in 1996 and is based on the true story of Grace Marks, a Canadian woman who was convicted of murder in the 19th century. The novel combines elements of historical fiction, crime and psychological drama.

The book is praised for its intricate storytelling, psychological aspects and exploration of societal issues. Margaret Atwood's skill in combining historical research with fiction
has contributed to the novel's critical and popular success.

6 The Grand Sophy

This is considered by many readers as one of Georgette Heyer's best Regency romances for its wit, the character of Sophy and the romantic tension between her and Charles. The novel was published in 1950 and is one of Heyer's most popular and enduring works. Heyer is known for her historical romance novels set in the Regency and Georgian periods, and *The Grand Sophy* is a delightful example of her witty and engaging storytelling.

7 A Farewell to Arms

Written by Ernest Hemingway, *A Farewell to Arms* draws on the author's own experiences fighting in World War 1. First published in 1929, the novel is known for its spare and understated prose, as well as its exploration of love, war and the impact of conflict on individuals.

The characters face adversity with a sense of dignity and resilience. Hemingway brings his journalistic experience to the prose, which is short and simple, making it an easy read despite the complex themes.

A Farewell to Arms is considered one of Hemingway's major works and is often praised for its poignant portrayal of the human experience in the face of war. The novel has been adapted into various films and stage productions and remains a classic in American literature.

8 A Passage to India

The 200 years of colonial rule in India has created a whole body of literature dealing with various aspects of the interactions between the British and Indians. *A Passage to India* is part of this canon. Written by English author E.M. Forster, it was published in 1924 and is set against the backdrop of British India in the early 20th century. The novel explores colonialism, cultural clashes and the complexities of human relationships, especially between the rulers and the ruled.

A Passage to India is considered one of Forster's masterpieces along with *Howard's End* and *A Room with a View.* The novel has been praised for its insightful exploration of cultural, political and personal complexities.

9 The Picture of Dorian Gray

This novel was written by Oscar Wilde and first published in 1890. *The Picture of Dorian Gray* tells the story of a young and handsome man in London, Dorian Gray, who sits for a portrait being painted by his friend, Basil Hallward. During the session, Dorian expresses the wish that he could remain young and beautiful while the portrait ages.

The novel explores themes of morality, the consequences of one's actions and the pursuit of pleasure and hedonism. It also delves into the darker aspects of human nature and the price one pays for indulging in a life without ethical constraints.

The novel is a masterpiece and a 19th century classic. It has been adapted into various films, plays and other forms of media. Its exploration of morality and aesthetics is classic Oscar Wilde.

10 The Adventures of Sherlock Holmes: The Blue Carbuncle

This volume, called *The Adventures of Sherlock Holmes*, published in 1892, houses various classic stories by Arthur Conan Doyle such as *The Red-Headed League*, *The Adventure of the Speckled Band* and *The Adventure of the Copper Beeches*, but *The Blue Carbuncle* stands out for the resolution of the mystery by the fictional detective Sherlock Holmes. *The Blue Carbuncle* has all the hallmarks of a classic Sherlock Holmes mystery such as deductive reasoning, attention to detail and the resolution of a seemingly complex case through logical analysis.

The character of Sherlock Holmes has left a lasting legacy in literature and popular culture. *The Blue Carbuncle* is among the many stories that have contributed to the enduring popularity of Holmes and his loyal companion, Dr. John Watson.

11 The Diary of Anne Frank

The poignant autobiographical account of a young Jewish girl, Anne Frank, who documents her experiences while hiding from the Nazis during World War II, *The Diary of Anne Frank* covers a period of over two years. From 1942 to 1944, Anne, her family and a few others lived in hiding in a secret annex above her father's office in Amsterdam, Netherlands, to escape Nazi persecution. It is considered one of the finest accounts of the world war period.

12 The God of Small Things

Arundhati Roy's *The God of Small Things* is set in the southern Indian state of Kerala and revolves around the lives of fraternal twins Estha and Rahel, who live with their mother Ammu and maternal grandparents Mammachi and Pappachi in their ancestral home, Ayemenem House.

The story is told through a series of flashbacks, jumping between past and present, but mostly through the viewpoint of Rahel, revealing the events that shaped the twins' lives. The central event of the novel is the visit of their English cousin, Sophie Mol, and her death.

The novel explores themes of love, family, social hierarchy and the rigid caste system. It delves into the complex relationships between the characters, including the twins' troubled relationship with their abusive and alcoholic father, Ammu's forbidden love affair with Velutha and the impact of manipulative relatives.

13 A Room of One's Own

Virginia Woolf's *A Room of One's Own* was first published in 1929. In the essay, Woolf explores the relationship between women and literature and their status in the literary world during the early 20th century. The title of the essay emphasizes the importance of space and autonomy for women writers—a physical and metaphorical room where they can practice their craft without the shackles of societal constraints.

A Room of One's Own is not only a critique of the gender biases inherent in the literary establishment but also a call to action for women to assert their creative agency and demand recognition for their talent. Through eloquent prose and analysis, Woolf continues to inspire writers to advocate for equality and empowerment in the literary world.

14 Persepolis: The Story of a Childhood Persepolis: The Story of a Return

Persepolis is a two-volume graphic memoir by Marjane Satrapi, published in 2000-2003 in French and 2003-2004 in English. It recounts Satrapi's childhood and early adulthood in Iran during and after the Islamic Revolution. The memoir is told through a series of black-and-white illustrations, combining personal anecdotes with historical events to provide an insight into life under a repressive regime and the complexities of identity, politics and culture.

15 The House of the Spirits

Isabel Allende's novel that became an instant bestseller when published in 1982 is inspired by Gabriel Garcia Marquez's *100 Years of Solitude*. The book deals with four generations of the Trueba family, delineating the social upheavals in post-colonial Chile. In 1993, the book was made into a movie starring Meryl Streep.

16 Beloved

Set against the background of the American Civil War, Toni Morrison's *Beloved* deals with a dysfunctional family that was formerly enslaved and whose home in Cincinnati is haunted by a malevolent spirit. The Pulitzer-winning novel has been dedicated to 'Sixty Million and More', referring to those who were killed because of the slave trade.

17 The Forty Rules of Love

Turkish author Elif Shafak was inspired to write this novel by her degree course in Gender and Women's Studies. Using the novel-within-a-novel technique, she blends two storylines set in modern day Britain and 13th century Turkey in a wonderful way that shows her mastery of writing.

AND MORE!

Of all the classics mentioned in this chapter, the one book that stands out has to be *Winnie-the-Pooh*. The book has never been out of print since it was first published in 1926 and had sold more than 20 million copies by the time Pooh bear turned 100 years old in 2024. Of course, it was an immediate success, having sold 35,000 copies in the U.K. and 150,000 copies in the U.S. by the end of the year it was first published.

Thanks to Disney, which acquired rights to the characters in 1961 from Steven Slesinger who had first taken Pooh and his friends out of the pages of the book into the world of merchandise and games in 1930, the characters became as familiar and famous as royalty and celebrities. In fact, Winnie-the-Pooh got his own star on the Hollywood Walk of Fame in 2006.

However, unlike the Mary Poppins books or Hans Christian Andersen's stories, which have been overtaken by Disney's super-loved animations, A.A. Milne's original works are still loved and read despite the glitz and glamour of Hollywood.

To celebrate Queen Elizabeth II's 90th birthday, Pooh bear ventured out of Hundred Acre Wood and went to Buckingham Palace, greeting the queen and her great-grandson Prince George and presenting her with a special hum song.

Ashwood Forest in Sussex, which inspired Hundred Acre Wood, was a deer-hunting forest and there is no indication that any bears ever lived there. Christopher Robin wasn't the biggest fan of his father's stories despite them having been inspired by his toys. Children at school used to tease him about *Winnie-the-Pooh*, and as Christopher got older, he felt that his father had earned his fame by standing on his son's shoulders.

The book has been translated into more than 50 languages including Latin. The 1958 Latin edition called *Winnie Ille Pu* became the first non-English book to be featured in the New York Times Bestseller List. Forbes magazine has ranked *Winnie-the-Pooh* as the second most valuable children's character after Mickey Mouse.

READiNG iN PROGRESS!

List the books you've read from the suggested lists!

Title ....

Author ....

Date completed ....

Title ....

Author ....

Date completed ....

Title ....

Author ....

Date completed ....

Title ....

Author ....

Date completed ....

Title ....

Author ....

Date completed ....

7

THE LiBRARY AT THE END OF THiS BOOK

Reading Spaces

No journey towards becoming a reader can be complete without libraries and reading spaces. Yes, it is great to build your own library, but no personal collection can compare with the resources offered by a good library.

Schools and universities offer libraries that are wonderful reading spaces. In primary schools especially, libraries are full of colour as they are designed to attract young readers. Libraries provide access to a vast collection of books, resources and services. Public libraries serve as community hubs, fostering a love for reading and lifelong learning. Libraries offer a quiet and peaceful environment for reading and studying, and many offer various programmes and events to engage the community in the act of reading.

Libraries certainly offer reading spaces but what about your home? Every home should have cozy nooks where you can curl up with a book. Creating a dedicated reading nook with comfortable seating and good lighting enhances the reading experience. Some people find solace in outdoor spaces like parks or gardens for reading.

By offering a diverse range of resources, programmes and events, libraries contribute significantly to the promotion of reading, literacy and a lifelong love for books in their community members through various activities.

1 Offering Extensive Book Collections

Libraries house extensive collections of books across various genres, catering to diverse interests and age groups. These collections encourage individuals to explore different literary works and discover new authors. There is no greater joy than browsing through rows and rows of shelves, searching for authors that you love to read.

2 Children's Storytime

Libraries often organize storytime sessions for young children, promoting early literacy and a love for books. Professional storytellers are scheduled to hold sessions for children where they use large picture books and puppets to narrate stories. These motivate children to search out the books from the library shelves.

3 Teen Reading Programmes

Libraries can come up with tailored reading programmes for teenagers to encourage them to engage with literature and foster a lifelong reading habit. This is much harder because the older the children, the more difficult it is to introduce them to reading and books. However, using interesting Young Adult books that have also been made into games, libraries can come up with gaming afternoons to draw in the reluctant teenager.

4 Adult Book Clubs

Libraries host book clubs for adults to discuss and share their thoughts on specific books, fostering a sense of community among readers. Such clubs are increasingly becoming popular especially among the older generation.

5 Author Events and Book Signings

Libraries frequently host author events, book readings and book signings. These events provide an opportunity for readers to meet their favourite authors, ask them questions on their loved books and also gain insights into the writing process. These are mutually beneficial as authors get direct feedback from the readers which is always valued by writers. Libraries actively promote local authors by featuring their works, organizing book launches and creating opportunities for the community to connect with writers from the region.

6 Reading Challenges

Libraries organize reading challenges that encourage participants to set reading goals, explore different genres or discover books from diverse perspectives. These challenges create a sense of accomplishment and motivation to read more. It also ensures that books remain in circulation justifying their purchase in the first place.

7 Literacy Programmes

Many libraries offer literacy programmes for individuals of all ages, including adult literacy initiatives. These programmes help improve reading and writing skills, empowering individuals to actively participate in society. Using their vast resources, libraries are able to organize such events across languages.

8 Offer Access to Digital Resources

In addition to physical books, libraries provide access to digital resources such as eBooks and audiobooks. This expands reading options and accommodates readers' diverse preferences. Libraries can also get rare resources through inter-library lending.

9 Community Engagement

Libraries engage with the local community by organizing book-related events, discussions and workshops. These activities create a vibrant literary culture and foster a sense of belonging among readers, making libraries interesting destinations for all age groups.

10 Accessible Spaces

Libraries provide welcoming and accessible spaces for reading, studying and contemplation. Comfortable seating, quiet reading areas and well-lit spaces enhance the overall reading experience.

11 Develop Partnerships with Schools

Libraries often collaborate with schools to support educational initiatives. They host book fairs, provide reading materials and facilitate library visits to instill a love for reading in students. School libraries may be good, but they have smaller budgets than the bigger common community libraries. By working together, they can ensure a bigger pool of books for students to choose from.

12 Pick and Choose

One of the best things about libraries is that no one judges you for choosing a different book. On top of that, in case you pick a book and ten pages in you're not invested, you can pick a different one and return the first one! That can't happen when it comes to a bookstore, can it? Libraries are therefore fertile grounds to experiment with your reading and figuring out what it is you like.

While libraries are perhaps the greatest place a reader can be to experience the brilliance of the written word, reading communities are also present in all their vibrancy and at their chatty best at other places and events.

Book Fairs

Book fairs are another place where booklovers can gather. It is where publishers, authors and readers come together to celebrate books. They provide an opportunity for book enthusiasts to discover new releases, meet authors and engage in literary discussions. Prominent book fairs include the New Delhi World Book Fair, Frankfurt Book Fair, London Book Fair and BookExpo America. The New Delhi World Book Fair held at Pragati Maidan since 1972 is the second-oldest book fair in the country after the Kolkata Book Fair. Organized by the National Book Trust (NBT), it is an annual event where publishers from across the world and the country gather to sign some of the biggest deals.

ACROSS THE COUNTRY, INDIA HOSTS NUMEROUS BOOK FAIRS, SOME DRAWING FOREIGN BOOKSELLERS AND AUTHORS IN LARGE NUMBERS.

The fair's importance is also because India is the third-biggest market for print books and the second-largest English-speaking economy. Apart from being home to the largest population at 1.4 billion, India has the largest population aged 5–24 years old in the world at 500 million people, and the largest school-going population at 265 million (according to 2022 data).

Across the country, India hosts numerous book fairs, some drawing foreign booksellers and authors in large numbers. These fairs are trade events but also host several events that are aimed at the masses such as author signings, book-related games, talks and seminars.

Apart from book fairs, bookstores are important in bringing the books closer to the consumers. Independent bookstores and large chains offer a wide selection of books, host author events and contribute to the local literary community.

Literary festivals which celebrate literature, featuring author talks, panel discussions, book signings and other literary activities supplement the book fairs. The most famous of these is the Jaipur Literature Festival which has now grown so big that it is held in other cities and even abroad such as at London and Houston.

Other prominent festivals include The Hindu Lit for Life, the Bangalore Literature Festival, the Apeejay Kolkata Literary Festival among others.

BOOK CLUBS ALSO SERVE A SIMILAR PURPOSE, BRINGING PEOPLE TOGETHER TO READ AND DISCUSS BOOKS.

Book Clubs

Online and local reading communities bring readers together to discuss books, share recommendations and participate in reading challenges. Platforms like Goodreads and online book clubs facilitate virtual discussions, while local book clubs allow face-to-face interactions.

Book clubs also serve a similar purpose, bringing people together to read and discuss books. They can be informal gatherings of friends or organized clubs with specific themes or genres. Book clubs foster a sense of community, provide diverse perspectives and encourage social interactions around literature.

Engaging with libraries, attending book fairs, exploring bookstores, participating in literary festivals and joining book clubs offer enriching experiences for bibliophiles, fostering a deeper connection to the world of books and reading.

The Frankfurt Book Fair, considered the oldest and largest book fair in the world, dates back to the 15th century. The first Frankfurt Book Fair took place in 1454, shortly after Johannes Gutenberg's invention of the movable-type printing press, making it an important event in the early history of book publishing.

The Frankfurt Book Fair was initially established as a trade fair for local booksellers. Over the centuries, it has evolved into an international marketplace for the publishing industry. Frankfurt's central location in Europe has contributed to its role as a hub for the global publishing community. The fair brings together publishers, authors, literary agents and book enthusiasts from around the world and serves as a platform for the buying and selling of publishing rights, promoting new releases and fostering international collaboration.

The Frankfurt Book Fair is known for its global reach, attracting exhibitors and visitors from various countries. It has become a major event for the exchange of ideas and the negotiation of book rights on an international scale. In recent years, the Frankfurt Book Fair has embraced the digital age, incorporating discussions on eBooks, digital publishing, and the impact of technology on the literary landscape.

The longevity and continued significance of the Frankfurt Book Fair makes it a key event on the literary calendar. It has played a crucial role in shaping the publishing industry and the world of books and literature.

BUiLD YOUR VOCABULARY!

List the new words you've read along with a short explanation.

8

HEART OF A BOOK

Reading For Life

With all the recommendations and lists of things to do to become a reader, you should be at least halfway towards becoming a reader by now. Hopefully you have also found the bonuses that come with reading.

One is that you start to develop more confidence in public and even large gatherings as you know you can hold your own in any discussion.

This confidence is not a small achievement. The by-product of this, a bonus if you will, is that you will find you are talking increasingly to people who are able to help you take the next step whether it be in your career or life goals.

Remember the episode of *Friends* called The One With The Cuffs where a man selling encyclopaedias knocks on the door while Joey is at home? The salesman's sales pitch is that Joey will never be caught out again when everyone is talking about something, and he has no idea about the topic and merely nods or laughs when the others laugh. Joey ends up buying one volume, the V volume, for $50 and feels intelligent when all his friends talk about the Vietnam war. But they move on to the Korean War and he is lost once again. That Joey with knowledge of the V volume is you but on a much larger scale. By becoming a reader, it is more or less like getting the advantage of possessing A to Z, the whole encyclopaedia of knowledge.

A LIFELONG PASSION FOR READING IS A JOURNEY THAT TRANSCENDS TIME, OPENING DOORS TO NEW WORLDS, DIVERSE PERSPECTIVES AND ENDLESS POSSIBILITIES.

For many, it begins as a spark in childhood, inspired by bedtime stories, fairytales and the comforting embrace of a parent's voice. As the pages turn, this initial fascination evolves into a lifelong love affair with books, weaving a tapestry of intellectual growth, emotional enrichment and a continuous quest for knowledge. It is a transformative odyssey, a passage that transcends the boundaries of time and space. The pages of books become entryways to fascinating worlds, windows into the human soul and bridges connecting disparate minds across the ages.

THE TEENAGER WHO iS A READER FINDS A CONFIDANT AND FRiEND iN EACH AND EVERY BOOK.

Teenage years bring a surge of curiosity and the reading palette broadens even further to cover a variety of genres. From fantasy and science fiction to classical literature and contemporary novels, young readers embark on a search, a quest for identity and understanding.

In the tumultuous adolescent years, when angst and anger are common, books become steadfast and dependable companions. The teenager who is a reader finds a confidant and friend in each and every book. The awkwardness of youth finds comfort in the stories that mirror their troubles, making the complexities of growing up easier to face and manage.

Literature becomes a silent confidant, offering empathy, understanding and a sanctuary where the reader can find refuge from the confusion of the external world. Books become mirrors reflecting the teenager's self and offering glimpses into the lives of others who might be going through the same feelings of angst.

In adulthood, the passion for reading takes on an even more multifaceted role. It becomes a means of intellectual stimulation, a tool for continuous learning and a catalyst for personal growth. Avid readers often find escape or refuge in literature during challenging times, turning to the written word for guidance, comfort or simply a way to deal with the pressures of the world. The booklover, now well-versed in the various genres, explores the vast world of literature eagerly. In fact, adulthood marks the zenith of the reader's journey – a time when the passion for books becomes a part of one's identity. Readers enjoy both fiction and non-fiction, like old friends who offer intellectual stimulation, emotional support and continuous companionship.

The bonus of a lifelong passion for reading is that the books you read evolve just as you do. As life unfolds and you change, so do your reading preferences. Reading becomes not just a hobby but a deliberate choice – you will find yourself carving out time even in the midst of a busy schedule to enjoy the written word. Because that is what it is – a joy, an enjoyment, not a chore. Whether it's the timeless classics that offer wisdom gained over the ages, contemporary works that mirror your life, or non-fiction books that provide insights into the world, the act of reading becomes something like a ritual that nurtures the mind and soul.

Once you become a reader and develop a love for books, you are never ever alone again. It is like getting a friend who goes everywhere with you. Books are the best friends you can have, almost like a dog's relationship with man.

"ONCE YOU'VE READ A BOOK YOU CARE ABOUT, SOME PART OF iT iS ALWAYS WiTH YOU."

LOUiS L'AMOUR

- prolific writer of western novels or what he called frontier stories

Yes, developing a love for books is like gaining a friend for life, but the act of reading is inherently social.

Book clubs, literary discussions and shared recommendations create communities of like-minded people who find joy in exploring narratives together. These communities become places where ideas are exchanged, where diversity is celebrated and where new connections are forged through the shared love of books. Every time booklovers gather, the solitary act of reading blossoms into a communal and social celebration of the written word.

In essence, reading is a dynamic activity that has an ever-unfolding narrative. It is a personal journey where each book, every page in fact, leaves an indelible mark on the reader's soul. From the innocence of childhood wonder to the wisdom of later years, the journey of a reader is proof of the enduring power of stories to shape, inspire and support us on the extraordinary voyage that is life. In every book that lines your bedroom and study shelves and every flicker of e-readers and iPads in the night, the passion for reading burns bright, a guiding light leading the way through life.

The act of reading transcends the mere consumption of words on a page; it is a dialogue with the essential human experience. Each book is a conversation with the author, an exchange of ideas across time and space in a way. Readers engage with characters who bear the weight of their own narratives, and in doing so, discover facets of themselves reflected in the pages of a book.

Bookstores and libraries become sacred spaces – a pilgrimage for booklovers. The scent of a book that has not yet been cracked open, the hushed whisper of pages as the reader turns them, the mesmerizing sight of shelves laden with books, all promise undiscovered worlds that are alluring and attractive. The acquisition of a new book is not merely a transaction but the first step into uncharted territories of the mind, a promise of hours of joy.

BOOKSTORES AND LIBRARIES BECOME SACRED SPACES—A PILGRIMAGE FOR BOOKLOVERS.

The booklover is booked for life; he understands that the reading journey is infinite. The to-be-read pile is an ever-expanding collection of promising possibilities, each book a star waiting to illuminate the reader's universe. The journey of a booklover is not a solitary path but a collective expedition, a testament to the enduring power of books and stories to bind, enlighten and shape a person.

In this grand narrative, the booklover is not a passive spectator but an active participant—a co-author of his or her own story, his or her own journey, practically booked for life.

1
THIRTEEN R3ASONS WHY EVERYONE SHOULD READ
A reader lives a thousand lives before he dies. The man who never reads lives only once.
- George R.R. Martin
2
FORTY RULES OF LOVING READING
How To Become A Book Lover
3
WALKING THROUGH READING WALLS
4
FIFTY SHADES OF BOOKS
Books over time
5
BOOK ENCHANTED
Starting Young
6
ONE HUNDRED YEARS OF READING
Book Recommendations
7
THE LIBRARY AT THE END OF THIS BOOK
Reading spaces
8
HEART OF A BOOK
Reading for life

THE READiNG CHALLENGE!

Here are some challenges that you can take on-

- ○ Read a book in translation
- ○ Read an animal story
- ○ Read a book from the 19th century
- ○ Read a war book

Add some more of your own:

MY 365-DAY BUCKET LiST

Sonali Bendre Behl is an award-winning Indian film actress, author and a passionate advocate of storytelling. She is the author of the candid and insightful *Modern Gurukul*, where she shares her experiences as a mother navigating modern parenting. Her enduring love for books inspired her to create Sonali's Book Club, a vibrant digital community celebrating literature and meaningful conversations.

She is now embarking on a new chapter in her writing journey, offering readers a thoughtful exploration of books and their profound impact on our lives.

ROHiNA THAPAR

Rohina is a design generalist, helping people and organizations build value through effective branding, communications and products. She has designed many books for children including the award-winning *Art is a Verb*, *Abanindranath's House of Stories*, *Art is a Voice* and *Ganesh Pyne's Twilight Dreams*. In 2023, she won the Kyoorius Design Award for the book design of *Eye Spy Indigenous Art*. She approaches her work as a self-reflective process and a quest to understand the bigger picture.

ACKNOWLEDGEMENTS

My thanks to:

- Sonali's Book Club team at 59th Parallel: Natasha Pal, Bhavna Tanwani and Khushi Bachwani

- HarperCollins and my publisher, Tina Narang

- Rohina Thapar for the brilliant design.

BUILD YOUR VOCABULARY!

FAVOURITES!

THE READING CHALLENGE!

CREATE YOUR OWN STORY!

READING IN PROGRESS!

MEMORIES OF
EADING AND BOOKS

READING LOG

HOW AND WHERE I READ

HarperCollins *Publishers* India

At HarperCollins India, we believe in telling the best stories and finding the widest readership for our books in every format possible. We started publishing in 1992; a great deal has changed since then, but what has remained constant is the passion with which our authors write their books, the love with which readers receive them, and the sheer joy and excitement that we as publishers feel in being a part of the publishing process.

Over the years, we've had the pleasure of publishing some of the finest writing from the subcontinent and around the world, including several award-winning titles and some of the biggest bestsellers in India's publishing history. But nothing has meant more to us than the fact that millions of people have read the books we published, and that somewhere, a book of ours might have made a difference.

As we look to the future, we go back to that one word—a word which has been a driving force for us all these years.

Read.

Harper Collins · 4th · HARPER FICTION · HARPER NON-FICTION · HARPER BUSINESS · HCCB HARPERCOLLINS CHILDREN'S BOOKS

HARPER DESIGN · Harper Sport · HARPER PERENNIAL · HARPER VANTAGE · हार्पर हिन्दी · BOOKTOPUS